THE SUNSET IN A CUP

Emily Dickinson and Mythopoeic Imagination

THE SUNSET IN A CUP

Emily Dickinson and Mythopoeic Imagination

Priyamvada Tripathi Anantharaman

COSMO PUBLICATIONS

NEW DELHI **INDIA**

1985

COSMO PUBLISHERS
Made in India

THE SUNSET IN A CUP

Published by :

Rani Kapoor (Mrs.)
COSMO PUBLICATIONS
24-B, Ansari Road,
Daryaganj, New Delhi

Printed at :

Swatantra Bharat Press,
Esplanade Road, Delhi-110 006

To my Mother
and
To the memory of my Father

Bring me the sunset in a cup,
Reckon the morning's flagon's up
And say how many Dew,
Tell me how far the morning leaps—
Tell me what time the weaver sleeps
Who spun the breadths of blue !

Write me how many notes there be
In the new Robin's extasy
Among astonished boughs—
How many trips the Tortoise makes—
How many cups the Bee partakes,
The Debauchee of Dews !

Also, who laid the Rainbow's piers,
Also who leads the docile spheres
By withes of supple blue ?
Whose fingers string the stalactite—
Who counts the wampum of the night
To see that none is due ?

Who built this little Alban House
And shut the window down so close
My spirit cannot see?
Who'll let me out some gala day
With implements to fly away
Passing Pomposity?

—Emily Dickinson

...*Poetry*

Exceeding music must take the place
Of empty heaven and its hymns,

Ourselves in poetry must take their place
Even in the chattering of your guitar.

—Wallace Stevens

ACKNOWLEDGMENTS

First and foremost, I am deeply beholden to the published Dickinson scholarship which has been tutoring and refining my critical faculties ceaselessly over the years. I still turn to Anderson, Chase, Sewall, Sherwood, Inder Nath, and Thackrey, when doubts and confusions cloud my mind Commentators and innovators like David Porter, Rebecca Patterson, Albert Gelpi, Sharon Cameron, R.W. Franklin, and Polly Longsworth, who are "traditional" (Suzanne Juhasz's adjective) and modern simultaneously in the annals of Dickinson criticism, by their continual effort to view Emily's poetry and life from several angles over the decades, have proved that the creative force and aesthetic appeal for her poems still stand undimmed and unspent. At the same time, but for Suzanne Juhasz emerging on the scene in the mid-seventies, and (with a score of others) so tenderly and devotedly refurbishing Dickinson scholarship with fine shades of feminist critical insights, an understanding of Emily as a "female poet" would have been inadequate. Though I differ considerably from the feminist literary critics in my approach to Dickinson, or to any other woman artist for that matter, the intensity and balance of my judgments owe much to them.

The voice that has provided authenticity, coherence, and monolithic structure to the central argument of the present book is Northrop Frye's. The beatitude of the critical visions provided by Frye is of such creative and consummate nature that one should like to write on him separately to unfold more fully the exegesis of his critical system.

I wish to take this opportunity to express my gratefulness to many friends, colleagues, and teachers, among them Pro-essors V. Rai, S.M. Pandeya, O.P. Mathur, Adappa Rama

Krishna and Dr. C.S. Singh, who encouraged and helped me at various stages of my work in innumerable ways. My heartfelt thanks to Professor Isaac Sequeria who with his charming generosity, took pains to go through and comment on an earlier draft of this book and drew my attention to many a critical slip and stylistic inaccuracy. His suggestions have added firmly to the refinement of the book. My discussions with Professors Douglas Gray and Susan Caldwell (the latter from Oklahoma, U.S.A.) at Rewley House, University of Oxford (U.K.), helped me in realising those subtleties of Dickinson's poetry which otherwise were beyond the range of my critical apperceptions.

I am grateful to Child's Memorial, Houghton, and Widener Libraries of Harvard University, U.S.A., for permitting me to use their Dickinson resources. My loving thanks to friends Roswitha and William Trayes of Rust Island, Massachusetts, for their magnanimous care and patience during the period of my intense preoccupation with Emily Dickinson at Harvard University, and for taking me on a visit to the Dickinson Homestead at Amherst.

The extremely kind and generous help of the library staffs of: John F. Kennedy Institut fuer Nordamerikastudien, Free University of West Berlin; the English Seminar Library and the Universitaetsbibliothek of Basel University (Switzerland); and Jones Library, Amherst (Mass.), deserves a special mention here. I am particularly indebted to American Studies Research Centre, Hyderabad (India) for great help and assistance I received there in collecting and assimilating the back ground critical material needed for my research project. My thanks are also due to American Centre Library, New Delhi; British Council Library, Calcutta; and Banaras Hindu University Library, Varanasi, for providing me relevant material on the subject readily and in time.

My appreciative thanks to Mr. P.K. Chatterjee and Mr. Patrick Jacob who typed the manuscript with commendable skill; and to Mr. Y. Satyanarayana who proofread the book for long and tiring hours.

I wish to record my sincere thanks to the University Grants Commission, New Delhi, and American Studies Research

Centre, Hyderabad, for financial assistance, which enabled me initially to work full time on Emily Dickinson.

The care and concern shown by the present A.S.R.C. Director, Dr. Luther S. Luedtke, at the very last moments of my work, left me moved and stunned. Where shall I find suitable words to express my gratefulness to his wife, a Dickinson *aficionado*, who quietly passed on to me (from her personal collection) the newest published book about what was happening in the lives of those who were closely associated with the poet. "And since it happened close to Emily Dickinson, it is important" (Richard B. Sewall in the "Preface" of the book).

Contents

INTRODUCTION

I

Emily Dickinson (1830-86) is a major American poet of the nineteenth century. Her poetry, however, came to the world in a facsimile fashion until 1955, when with T.H. Johnson's variorum edition, we had an authentic text of the entire body of her poetry, with all its variants given by the poet. Since that date, Emily Dickinson has been ushered as a "poet restored," and a "discovery of the twentieth-century critics." The post-World War II critics in America and abroad have shown a slow, sustained, and steady interest in Emily Dickinson's life as well as poetry. But, for reasons partly ascribable to her singularly cloistered life which shunned all human relations and social contracts beyond its orbit, and partly to the obscurity and obliqueness of the verses, her poems could not get the attention and estimate they deserved. A *poetry*, so refreshingly modern in its style and technique, and universal in the spectrum of its themes, is still awaiting serious critical attention, objective and unbiased, which is inspired by the promise of the *poetic truth* in its absoluteness, and not by the pull of *biographical extravaganza* with all its enticements. This book is a consciously cultivated effort in this direction.

As it is, the poems have been studied as poems, and analysed with the help of the insights gathered from Emily Dickinson's poetry, letters, and other random statements and not from her life-history. The broad structure of Dickinson's poetic imagination, which is essentially mythopoetic, has been examined by a close textual analysis of some of her leading poems. The chapters have been divided thematically. In the Introduction here I will survey Dickinson scholarship since the first publication of her poems (1890) to the present day,* with an emphasis on the main critical trends.

In the subsequent chapters, Dickinson's poems divided under thematic heads have been examined, analysed, and discussed in detail. The book in the end turns to discuss Emily Dickinson's non-conformist personality, and compare it with the celebrated non-conformism of Huckleberry Finn. In conclusion I have attempted to put across the results and important findings of my close textual study of Dickinson's poetry.

II

Charles R. Anderson has reminded us that to give Emily Dickinson's poetry "the serious attention it deserves is the real task that remains. To study it intensively, to stare a hole in the page until these apparently cryptic notations yield their full meanings—this is the great challenge to modern readers."[1] The challenge still remains unanswered, in spite of the fact that several attempts at a study of Emily Dickinson's life and poetry have been made by scholars such as Clark Griffith,[2] Jay Leyda,[3] Albert J. Gelpi,[4] Ruth

*Between the completion of the manuscript of the present book (1979), and its publication (1985), an exciting new era in Dickinson criticism not only started at the annual meetings of the Modern Language Association (1978 and 1979), but reached its socholarly Zenith in 1983 with the publication of Suzanne Juhasz's splendid collection of feminist essays on Emily Dickinson. In the meanwhile, R.W. Franklin's solidly researched and cautiously documented two volumes of the Manuscript Books of Emily Dickinson (1981) heralded a new accomplishment in the history of Dickinson criticism. In both these cases, the follow up studies have not been less important. The impact of these modernist trends on Dickinson scholarship is bound to be far-reaching, and I feel my book will be incomplete, and my argument injudicious, if I do not evaluate and summarise the intrinsic worth of these critical trends in my present work. An *Afterword* at the end of the book does that *a priori.*

[1]Charles R. Anderson, "Preface," *Emily Dickinson's Poetry: A Stairway of Surprise* (Garden City: Doubleday & Co., Anchor Books, 1969), p. xiv.

[2]Clark Griffith, *The Long Shadaw: Emily Dickinson's Tragic Poetry* (Princeton : Princeton University Press, 1964).

[3]Jay Leyda, *The Years and Hours of Emily Dickinson,* 2 Vols. (New Haven : Yale University Press, 1969).

[4]Albert J. Gelpi, *Emily Dickinson: The Mind of the Poet* (Cambridge, Mass : Harvard University Press, 1965).

Miller,[5] Richard Chase,[6] Jack L. Capps[7], and Brita Lindberg-Seyersted.[8]

Inder Nath Kher's study of Emily Dickinson[9] is laboriously welded with opinions. Kher explores Dickinson's poetry with a view to grasping her "spiritual biography" and the place of "terror" in it. A close analysis of her poems is done at some length to demonstrate the presence of "terror," "perception," and elements of "spiritual biography" in her poetry. Within these limits, Kher's attempt at an intensive study of Emily Dickinson is laudable.

Ever since the publication of the first series of her poems in 1980, biographers and critics have shown a curious interest in this "private" poet. She was not a "self critic" like Wordsworth or Coleridge, and hated publication as "the auction of man's mind." She hardly left anything in its final stage, fit for publication. Emily Dickinson has appealed to her readers as an elusive figure. T.W. Higginson writes :

> I saw her but twice, face to face and brought away the impression of something as unique and remote as Undine or Mignon or Thekla.[10]

When Higginson moved from person to poetry, his comments were equally subjective and equivocal :

> Her verses are like poetry pulled up by the roots, with rain, dew and earth still clinging, giving a freshness and fragrance not otherwise conveyed.[11]

---

[5]Ruth Miller, *The Poetry of Emily Dickinson* (Middletown, Conn.: Wesleyan University Press, 1968).

[6]Richard Chase, Emily Dickinson (New York : William Sloane Associates, 1951).

[7]Jack L. Capps, *Emily Dickinson's Reading* : 1836-86 (Cambridge, Mass : Harvard University Press, 1966).

[8]Brita Lindberg-Seyersted, *The Voice of the Poet* : *Aspects of Style in the Poetry of Emily Dickinson* (Cambridge, Mass : Harvard University Press, 1968).

[9]Inder Nath Kher, *The Landscape of Absence* : *Emily Dickinson's Poetry* (New Haven : Yale University Press, 1974).

[10]Thomas Wentworth Higginson, "Preface," *Poems by Emily Dickinson* (Boston : Roberts Brothers, 1890).

[11]*Ibid.*

Or, "if she had mastered the rudiments of grammar and gone into metrical training for about fifteen years, she might have been an admirable lyric poet of the second magnitude. Pulling up the roots is a very poor way to treat either flowers or poetry."[12]

There were some, however, who recognized her greatness; there were readers enough to buy sixteen printings of the first edition within nine years. She was treated rather as a poet of delicacy and charm, almost a "keepsake poet", as the format of her first volume with its Indian pipes on the cover seemed to present her. This was the first phase of Dickinson criticism, and Emily was accepted by her readers as a popular poet ; there was little or no critical attention. Then, a few years passed in total vacuum (1900-1913). In 1914 the second phase started with her niece Martha Dickinson Bianchi publishing another series of her poems, and preparing the ground for subsequent endeavours of critics. Dolores Dyer Lucas has called these endeavours "the psychic-wand approach."[13]

In this phase a fashion to give imaginative variations of Emily's poems started, an emphasis, which reached its peak in Rebecca Patterson's *The Riddle of Emily Dickinson* (*1951*). The publication of *Bolts of Melody* (*1945*) was another significant milestone in the flurry of Dickinson criticism. This volume wore marks of editorial precision, and the need of a definitive edition was immediately felt. Aiken and Tate had already taken Emily Dickinson seriously as a poet. Whicher's[14] and H.W. Wells's[15] full length books, though superseded now, were a commendable effort in view of the fragmentary state of materials they could lay their hands on. Henry Wells is, in fact, among the first few critics who studied Emily Dickinson's diction, verbal-patterns, sentence-structures, and

[12]Thomas Bailey Aldrich, *The Atlantic Monthly*, 69 (January 1892), 143.

[13]Dolores Dyer Lucas, "Introduction," *Emily Dickinson and Riddle* (Illinois : Northern Illinois University Press, 1969), p. 5.

[14]George Frisbie Whicher, *This Was a Poet : A Critical Biography of Emily Dickinson* (New York : Charles Scribner's Sons, 1938).

[15]Henry W. Wells, *Introduction to Emily Dickinson* (Chicago : Packard and Co., 1947).

major themes seriously. Donald Thackrey's[16] essay is a superb example of "pre-restoration" textual criticism, which was virtually non-existent at that time.

Then came T. H. Johnson's definitive variorum edition (1955), and with it greater emphasis was deservedly placed on her poetry. This Harvard edition of her poetry became, in fact, the harbinger of the "restoration" of Emily Dickinson as a person, and also as a poet. "The restoration," Richard B. Sewall concludes, "brought a new text, new letters, a chronology that provided at least a working basis for discussion and a host of new peripheral, and some central, data."[17]

Exciting new investigations into the poet's life, poetry, and literary resources were now underway. Her letters were now described as her "conversation", and autobiography was given much the same importance as her poetry. Jack L. Capps studied literary allusions in her verse, and presented convincing evidence that "an entire poem frequently turns upon an enigmatic allusion that becomes meaningful when related to her reading."[18]

In 1955 came Millicent Todd Bingham's[19] thorough documentation of Emily Dickinson's life, from which Emily Dickinson's family relationships, home life, and friendships could be understood in a new light. In Mrs. Bingham's book, the chapter called "The making of a Home" is especially interesting and revealing. The then current myth of Emily Dickinson as the Moth of Amherst "mediating majestically among her flowers" (Jay Leyda's parody of the poet) is exploded, and we see Emily Dickinson living a normal work-a-day life in a New England Puritan Household. T.H.

---

[16]Donald E. Thackrey, *Emily Dickinson's Approach to Poetry* (Lincoln : University of Nebraska Press, 1954),

[17]Richard B. Sewall, ed., *Emily Dickinson : A Collection of Critical Essays*. (Englewood Cliffs, New Jersey : Prentice-Hall, 1963), Introduction, p. 2.

[18]Jack L. Capps, *Emily Dickinson's Reading : 1836-86* (Cambridge, Mass : Harvard University Press, 1966), pp. vii-viii.

[19]Millicent Todd Bingham, *Ancestors' Brocades : The Literary Debut of Emily Dickinson* (New York : Harper & Bros,, 1945).

Johnson's[20] interpretive biography, which came the same year, established Emily Dickinson as "direct, impulsive and original," living in her three worlds simultaneously, and "making them the substance of everything that she thought and wrote." The three worlds were these : there was the world of nature, the things and creatures that she saw, heard, and felt about ; there was the "estate"—that is the world of friendship ; and there was the world of the unseen and the unheard, whence we "trail clouds of glory."

In 1960 Jay Leyda[21] cleared much of the controversy concerning Dickinson and provided valuable material for subsequent studies. In his two-volume monumental work, he refabricated Dickinson's life strictly with the help of existing documents of the poet, and other printed sources. His essentially chronological approach has led Leyda to come to a significant conclusion that "the riddle, or the deliberate omission of a circumstance too well-known to need repeating, was a major device of both Emily Dickinson's letters and her poetry."[22] To study Emily Dickinson's biography, one need not go beyond Leyda, and with *The Years and Hours of Emily Dickinson*, "What Leyda has called," to quote Richard B. Sewall,[23] "*the late haw of a frozen image* was complete."

Textually, the 1955 variorum edition brought the renaissance of Dickinson criticism. We finally had poems of Emily Dickinson substantially as she wrote them, though, in full agreement with Anderson, one would say that some difficult questions were still unanswered. It is, however, a different side of the story that my questions and doubts point to questions different from Anderson's.[24] Anderson is more concerned with the editing part of the text, whereas interesting questions are suggested by Sewall,[25] who has his reservations about seeing the poet *developmentally* since the dating of her

[20]Thomas H. Johnson, *Emily Dickinson, An Interpretive Biography* (Cambridge, Mass : Harvard University Press, Belknap Press, 1955).

[21]Jay Leyda, *The Years and Hours of Emily Dickinson*, 2 Vols. (New Haven : Yale University Press, 1960).

[22]Jay Leyda, p. xxi.

[23]Richard B. Sewall, "Introduction," *Emily Dickinson*, p. 2.

[24]Charles R. Anderson, p. x.

[25]Richard B. Sewall, p. 2.

poems can only be approximate, and therefore, different phases of her career cannot be neatly articulated.

Sewall has very competently revealed how the Harvard edition with its variants helped the reader in determining the occasional nature of many of the poems, inserted in letters or quoted otherwise. Also, for the first time in the annals of Dickinson criticism, a "typographical approximation" of her punctuation was attempted, and it was established that her unpredictable use of dashes cannot be dismissed as eccentric and unjustified—as the uniformity of the manuscript warrants it. She could not have used the dashes so often throughout her entire poetry, without meaning them. Emily Dickinson's editors have always been puzzled by her punctuation, with her seemingly erratic capitalization and prodigal use of dashes, though they varied in length and slant (some tilted up, some down, some horizontal). For the most part, the early editors simply "corrected" the eccentric poet's punctuation.

T.H. Johnson, however, with his scholarly respect for and fidelity to the text, corrected the obvious misspellings and misplaced apostrophes. Punctuation and capitalization remained unaltered. Johnson concludes that Dickinson uses dashes as a musical device, as "they frequently become visual representations of a musical beat."[26] The music of the poet's lines parallels the handling of her imagery in exquisite modulations of basic simplicity.

Johnson has fully examined how she used the meter of her church hymnal, most frequently following the common hymn measure of eight and six syllables, but often setting up patterns of long meter, (8, 8, 8, 8), short meter (6, 6, 8, 6), common particular meter (8, 8, 6,8, 8, 6), and so on. Yet just as she made her individual interpretations and denials of the doctrines of her church, so also she did not hesitate to bend the hymn meters to suit her own medium.

---

[26]Thomas H. Johnson, "Introduction," *The Poems of Emily Dickinson*, in 3 Vols. (Cambridge, Mass. The Belknap Press of Harvard University Press, 1963), p. lxiii. In subsequent references, this source will

From hymnology, from Emerson, and from Elizabeth Barrett Browning, she received a "training" for practicing inexact rhyme ; but no other poet, before the twentieth century, had so fully exploited the effects of inexact rhyme as she did. To take a random example, in the poem "After great pain, a formal feeling comes," there are six rhymes, but only three are conceivably exact ; the other three (comas-Tombs ; round-ought ; head-outlived) show the oblique quality in rhyme that characterizes her poetry.

Edith Wylder[27] has found that Emily's notation signs followed a consistent pattern of tonal or pitch stresses. The effect of the Harvard edition of her poetry has been such that some fresh approaches have been stimulated. These have established her as a major poet in the English language. She is greeted as a discovery of the twentieth century critics. There is little or no dispute about her stature as a poet, though the final dimensions of her poetic genius are still undecided.

The attitude expressed in most of Emily Dickinson's poetry is closer to what we choose to call modern than to the general conception of what people were thinking in the eighteen-nineties. The flippancy of many of her religious poems, her epigrammatic brevity, and unexpected mingling of sardonic wit with sentiment, find numerous parallels in the work of our contemporary poets. And, therefore, the modern critics have claimed her as their own. It still remains, however, to determine the exact nature of her poetic achievement.

The greatest achievement of the Harvard edition has been that quite a few serious textual studies have come out, studies which were not possible earlier. Magazines devoted to explication of poems have substantially contributed to good textual studies of her poems in the form of short analytical essays. The first full-length textual study was Anderson's, which analyzed about a hundred poems with precision, and in detail. Johnson for the first time analyzed Dickinson's use of hymn measures. Reeves, after a close examination of her poems, perceptively concludes: "We

---

[27]Edith Wylder, *The Last Face : Emily Dickinson's Manuscripts* (Alburquerque : University of New Mexico Press, 1971).

have to do with a poet of almost total originality and it is very rarely that originality and formal perfection go together."[28]

Owing to complex biographical-textual-critical problems surrounding Emily, the tendency has always been to single out and emphasize a certain aspect of her : for example, the life as opposed to the poetry, or, more recently, the letters as opposed to the life and poetry. On account of these several emphases which have emerged out of the body of studies now in process, a reconciliation of her life and lyrics may be one direction the criticism might take. Allen Tate has remarked : "There is none of whom it is truer to say that the poet is the poetry."[29]

III

The large body of Emily Dickinson's poetry may seem unexplained when seen in the light of the narrow circle of her life. One of the three children of a leading lawyer in Amherst, she lived an unexceptional girlhood in its experiences and enthusiasms. Her image, for many people, has been one of a sensational mixture of sentiment and romance. She is viewed as one who fell in and out of love with several men. A very different portrayal of her has been that of the "New England Nun"—a dedicated artist—shy, cloistered, fugitive perhaps, but one who selected a way of life as deliberately as she chose a metaphor.

Intense, cryptic, paradoxical, her life had a unity of purpose that battled to achieve and reveal a universal experience. None of the many explanations which have been offered for her "carefully obliterated life" can be accepted as entirely satisfactory. "I remember a tree in McLean Street, when you and we were a little girl, whose leaves went topsy-turvy as often as wind, and showed an ashen side—that's fright, that's

[28] James Reeves, "Introduction," *Selected Poems of Emily Dickinson* (New York : The Macmillan Co., 1959).

[29] Allen Tate, "Emily Dickinson," *Collected Essays* (Denver : The Swallow Press, 1932).

Emily."[30]

The tone of the passage just quoted confirms the speaker as a child, innocent and naughty, and not a precocious one. Emily Dickinson, a New England woman of the mid-nineteenth century, had a limited choice in the absence of marriage. She could be a teacher, a graceful family hostess, a recluse, a poet or she could choose the career of a perpetual child. She deliberately chose to be the last three, not one at a time, but all in one. She was very well suited for this last role. Such an assumption is warranted as much by her poems as by her letters. One may now turn from her mortal biography to her poetic biography; to call it her' 'spiritual biography," as Inder Nath Kher does, is not so exact unless things imagined can be included in it.

Why do critics try to dissolve Emily Dickinson's poetry in her biography ? Because they fail to find the convincing sources of her imagination anywhere else than in her perso na life and her so-called love-affairs. Here the problem is not exactly Shakespearean, for there are people who say that Shakespeare did not write Shakespeare's plays. Since biographical critics are convinced that literature is produced out of personal experiences, they have a problem with Shakespeare, whose life is not well known.

Biographical critics forget or simply ignore T.S. Eliot's statement that there is always a difference between the man who suffered, and the mind which created—that literature is not a product of direct experience, but a restructuring of the experience in imaginative language. Art, according to Plato, is a dream for awakened minds, a work of imagination withdrawn from ordinary life. Although art is dominated by the same forces that dominate dream, it gives us a perspective of reality that we do not get from any other approach to it.

Emily Dickinson imaginatively creates her poetic experiences around certain symbols derived out of her life and reading, out of the bees, bobolinks, and flowers of her garden,

[30]*The Letters of Emily Dickinson*. ed., Thomas H. Johnson, Vol. II (Harvard University Press, 1958), p. 264. In subsequent chapters, Dickinson's letters will be referred to as ...to be followed by the volume number and the letter number.

or deaths she witnessed and friendships she lived. All these imaginatively created experiences represent an order of reality and stability, death and rebirth to a new life. This imaginative creation of an experience is an evidence of the myth-making power of her mind, which throws up and dissolves one system or one experience and evolves a new one. This is why she is preoccupied with the theme of death and brands up immortality as her "flood subject."

Emily was a poet, and her work, like that of other poets, changed and at times got conditioned by her life-events. Her greatest poems are written in a form, classical in its condensation, which she evolved for herself, and for the most part managed so skillfully that, in spite of its lack of technical precision, it rarely failed to respond to the demands put upon it by the mythopoeic faculty in her. As a sensitive woman, she passed through emotional history so complicated, so intense, and mostly so triumphant, that the lack of any record of its course and its development can only be viewed as a real deprivation. There are a number of things in her poetry that demand to be set against the background of the poet's life in order to be intelligible. And that setting is not far away, thanks to the efforts of a host of biographical critics of Emily Dickinson.

The concentration of the present study, therefore, will not be on Emily Dickinson's biography, but on her changing approach to reality *as a poet*, for whom poetry was not so much a means of self-expression, as it was a means of probing and analyzing the existence she was to lead. To Sherwood's basic assumption that poetry is a form of autobiography,[31] Sirkka Heiskanen Makela's reply is acceptable to me; it is very perceptive: "Poetry is more than autobiography, it is myth; the realization on virtual, symbolic level of language of all the poet's potential faculties of experience."[32]

What I find important is not the circumstances out of

---

[31]Quoted in William R. Sherwood, *Circumference and Circumstance* (New York; Columbia University Press, 1968).

[32]Sirkka Heiskanen Makela, *In Quest of Trust*; *Observations on the Development of Emily Dickinson's Poetic Dialectic* (Jyvaskyla ;

which Dickinson's poetry seems to have been born, but the emerging pattern of the *imaginative experience* of life which goes far beyond the circumstances, and finds in them, at best, only an affirmation, and not an explanation of itself. Her concern is with the reality of the poetic vision, a reality which is neither totally subjective, nor totally objective, but brought into being through creation itself as an act of her mythopoeic mind. She comes very close to no other literary artist, among her predecessors, than Blake, whose concern is more or less the same as Emily's. To have a clue from Northrop Frye,[33] her peculiar manner of developing personally relevant symbols—a whole symbology—is typically Blakean.

A proper criticism of Emily Dickinson's poetry can, therefore, be attempted with an eye to its synthesizing process. One can start with the assumption that it is a singular mythopoeic poetry, having a single archetypal structure as its literary quality, extending from centre to circumference. Emily Dickinson's remark that the Bible deals with the centre and "my business is circumference" can be adopted as a heuristic principle for unwrapping the concealed dimensions of her poetry. We have to view her "centre" and "circumference" as the major components of her literary symbolism —as the larger contexts for categorizing and interpreting her poems.

Once our view of her big terms, "Centre," "Circumference," "Immortality," "Awe," "Love," "Nature," and "Death" comes into proper focus, many of her ambiguous poems will naturally reveal their meaning. We shall first concern ourselves with her notion of the centre.

In the poet's ordinary state of consciousness there is an enormous gap between herself and the world, a world set over against her. Almost all her poems undertake a quest for a complete identification between the subject and the object, imagination and reality. Since this quest is a poetic quest, its logic is the logic of metaphor and imagination, not of doctrine. The states and symbols of this quest of the imagination are mainly four : Centre, Circumference, Awe, and Death. The metaphors of the Centre and Circumference are

[33]Northrop Frye, *The Fables of Identity* Introduction, (New York: Harcourt, Brace and World, Inc., 1963). p. x.

drawn from the Circle. The Centre is followed by Circumference, which induces a recognition of God as the innermost secret of human consciousness. Then the different moods such as that of an identification with Nature or an intense Love experience follow. These are ultimately superceded by Death and subsequent stages of Awe, the invisible presence of the Holy Spirit, in Immortality and Eternity. But Emily Dickinson remains a sceptic till the very end and believes in the doctrine of "earth is heaven," "whether heaven is heaven or not" she does not know.

Except the Heaven had come so near—
So seemed to choose My Door—
The Distance would not haunt me so—
I had not hoped—before—
But just to hear the Grace depart—
I never thought to see—
Afflicts me with a Double Loss—
'Tis lost—And lost to me— (J. 472)

A simple commonsense paraphrase of the poem will run something like this : "I would never have felt such an acute sense of loss if Heaven, or Grace, had not made Himself felt so close to me and then departed." The narrator feels the distance between herself and Grace so vast now because He had come so near. The sense of deprivation now is doubly intense because of her having found, for once, a near identity with Grace. For, the more valuable the experience, the greater the sense of deprivation at the loss of it. Again, the near identity with Grace was something she never hoped to achieve, had never even thought of seeing. Grace came to her of its own accord. This means that she was surprised and stunned with joy by Grace. The intensity of joy lay in having attained what she had not thought herself to be worthy of. All this makes her sense of loss at the departure of Grace doubly intense.

But it is possible to interpret this brief poem in a variety of ways depending on the ingenuity of the interpreter. One may say that the first two lines of the poem bristle with ambiguity, for poem verges on the border of riddle, as the speaker does on the border of heaven. There are poems in which neither the identity of the persona is quite clear, nor the cardinal points of the poetic thought easily graspable. Such poems are usually ignored by the critics. But a critical approach worth its salt must grapple with the problems. It cannot avoid them, though the critics suppress such poems.

Some of Emily Dickinson's poems may be interpreted as conveying the experience of a mental traveller who at the end of the journey discovers that the achievement of the actual sojourn in the world of physical reality is not so fascinating as the idea of it seems—and then, the traveller is trapped in the dilemma of "to be or not to be." In the end the triumph of reaching the end aimed at is there, though the attained object disappears, leaving the traveller with a sense of loss, although expressed in a gay and glorious mood.

This, of course, is an oversimplification of Emily's poetic thought, but it has got to be done as the first step in analysis. In the poem quoted above who had "come so near"? And who "seemed to choose" the narrator's door? Obviously, Heaven, or Grace. The poem talks of the "distance" from the point of view of the narrator. "The Distance would not haunt me so—/ I had not hoped—before—." Some of Emily's poems have the quality of a riddle about them : and like all riddles they have the "middle ground ambiguity," that is, "the victim can retort that by the stated terms there can be more than one answer."[34]

Heaven, or Grace, was one of the needs of Emily.[35] Grace is the holy spirit, deity of Heaven—"And Grace would grant the Pair." It is synonymous with the "Great Spirit." : "Great

[34]Paull F. Baum, trans., *Anglo-Saxon Riddles of the Exeter Book* (Durham N.C. : Duke University Press, 1963), p.x. According to Baum, "Riddles belong to that large family of expressions in which something is represented as something else... A resemblance is stated as implied... But in the riddle there is an element of calculated deception ; the resemblance is submerged in deliberate ambiguity or obscurity." Baum analyzes that there are types of ambiguity present in a riddle—a riddle may be a powerful exercise in intelligence, it can be an exercise of wits—a kind of game and the third is the "middle ground ambiguity," in Baum's terms, which, we can add, we find in Emily Dickinson's poems.

[35]In a poem, Emily Dickinson says : "I meant to have but modest needs—/ Such as content—and Heaven—. (J. 476).

Spirit—Give to me/A Heaven not so large as Yours, But large enough—for me—" (J. 476). Grace goes away, leaving the narrator stunned with a sense of loss. The feeling of loss is conveyed penetratingly through the technique of repetition : " 'Tis lost—And lost to me—."

The emphasis in any analysis of Emily's poetry, and for that matter of any poem, should fall on the formal constituents of the poems, and on how they express the poet's theme. One may make use of the biographical and historical background to throw light on the meaning of a poem whenever it can help elucidation. In my own study of Emily's poetry the emphasis will fall on what and how her poems convey the imaginative experience and meaning. She herself believed in telling all the truth but telling it "slant" ; she considered the success of a poem residing in its circuitous expression. Each of her poems will be treated as a self-contained entity.

The circumstances that led to a poem's composition, and a knowledge of the poet's life, though interesting in themselves, cannot account for its effect. An overemphasis on the personal life of the poet shifts our attention from the poem to something that is not she poem. Art is not a parasite on the artist's life, but seeks its perfection through his talent. To understand Keats's "Ode to A Nightingale" it is not necessary to know that Keats, shortly before writing the poem, actually did witness the death of his younger brother. And if for a precise understanding of the poem such information becomes absolutely necessary and unavoidable it will mean that the poet has failed to universalize the experience and the poem may be viewed as a failure. A successful poem becomes independent of the feeding tubes of the poet's ego. Dickinson's poems on "Wild nights' or ' Cigar Smoking" may very easily lead a biographical critic to glib speculations. Wordsworth as a poet was highly sensitive to the experiences of his childhood and early youth which, he was equally aware, would diminish in the passing years.

When we come to Emily Dickinson, her announcement that her business is with the circumference has a bearing on her poetry. In her thirties composing poems became an integral part of her existence. Her preoccupation with the circumference of reality, the human consciousness, was a conscious and deliberate act of perception which conditioned her entire poetic career. It is for this reason that we should try to understand the major body of her poetry as an organized expression of the adventures of her imagination or, if one prefers, her transcendental consciousness. Poetry, for Emily, no more remains an instance of an experience taken over from the gross physical reality and rendered objectively or subjectively as in discursive writing. It becomes something which narrows down steadily and surely the sense of duality between the experience and the imagination. It is through Emily's art that the imaginative experience becomes available to the reader.

When, Emily remarked, on reading a poem, she cold feel that the top of her head was blown off, or she was frozen to a point where no fire could warm her, she knew it was genuine poetry ; she emphasized that a poem's effect was the only way though which she knew poetry. She considered the intensity of effect on the reader to be the test of a good poem. But, actually speaking, the intensity of effect is not a very reliable criterion of sound poetry. What the reader should rely on is not the intensity of the direct experience, but an understanding of the poem.

As to the background of Emily's poetry, I consider the period of its composition, ending with her death at the age of fifty-six, to be an important reference point. The second important thing, which I have already taken note of, is the period of its publication and critical appraisal, extending from 1890 till the present.* Everyone knows details of the second period, not fully well though ; for it is a period of uncertainties, disappointments, speculations and, until the 1955 variorum edition, of editorial manipulations and confusions. It is, however, the first period, the years of poetic composition, that is of real importance. Interpretations and revelations of facts about the period of composition are still inconclusive and largely conjectural. The poems, letters, and other documents brought together, however, make now a good lighthouse.

A few intriguing questions concerning her biography still

*See note on page one and two.

remain to be answered by scholarship. Why were only six poems published during her lifetime, and those too without a mention of the poet's name ? Why did she initiate correspondence with T.W. Higginson in her late twenties or early thirties, and sought literary advice from him only to flout it eventually? Was she not singularly aware and sure of her poetic talents and her destiny as a poet? Did she, or did she not, know with a fair degree of certainty that one day she would be accepted and acclaimed on her own uncompromising terms, and so she need not bring herself round to the poetic idiom of the day? Again, why did she develop fear of "froglike" publicity? How is it that the singleness of purpose in writing intense, unconventional verses remained with her until the very end? Was her devotion and dedication to poetry really guided by frequent emotional frictions during the last twenty or twenty-five years of her life? Did she fight with real emotional upheavals of life by channelizing them into verse, or did she have perfect artistic control over her emotions ? A few of the poems give a clue to her own view of some of these questions :

To fight aloud, is very brave—
But *gallanter*, I know
Who charge within the bosom
The Cavalry of Woe—

Who *win*, and nations do not see—
Who fall—and none observe—
Whose dying eyes, no Country
Regards with patriot love—

We trust, in plumed procession
For such, the Angels go—
Rank after Rank, with even feet—
And Uniforms of Snow. (J. 126)

I can wade Grief—
Whole Pools of it—
I'm used to that—
But the least push of Joy
Breaks up my feet—
And I tip—drunken—
Let no Pebble—smile—
'Twas the New Liquor—
That was all!

Power is only Pain—
Stranded, thro' Discipline,
Till Weights—will hang—
Give Balm—to Giants—
And they'll wilt, like Men—
Give Himmaleh—
They'll Carry—Him : (J. 252)

After great pain, a formal feeling comes—
The Nerves sit ceremonious, like Tombs—
The stiff Heart questions was it He, that bore,
And Yesterday, or Centuries before ?

The Feet, mechanical, go round—
Of Ground, or Air, or Ought—
A Wooden way
Regardless grown,
A Quartz contentment, like a stone—

This is the Hour of Lead—
Remembered, if outlived,
As Freezing persons, recollect the Snow—
First—Chil—then Stupor—then the letting go —(J. 341)

It is clear from these poems that Emily had a perfec artistic control over the emotions which she uses as the materials out of which her poems are made. Even if these were her personal emotions, she had the required capacity to withdraw from them, detach herself from herself, in order to work at them with a craftsman's detachment, without which art is not possible. Again, she universalizes the emotions and experiences she expresses.

We have enough documents available now to unravel the mystery of so many searching questions touching her life and art. Although she has left behind no formal preface to bring forth her theories of poetry, some of them can be gleaned from her verses themselves, and many more from her letters and other documents if fitted together into a proper relationship. The revisions she made of her poems were extensive, and she worked and reworked on them. And that testifies to her being a conscious artist : she might have been anticipating the publication of her poems some day. Though the data for biographical appraisal are extensive, the factual basis for much of her poetry still remains highly improbable.

One can, however, hopefully look forward to solving some of the questions. How did her reading shape her growth ? What books and authors did she really value and let herself be under their influence ? What were the personal influences from outside her family circle that determined her lifestyle and thought ? The impact of the friendship of young lawyer Benjamin F. Newton, and his premature death, is of course deep and definite in giving direction to her career as an artist; but what and how, nobody knows. In her mature years, there was a remarkable, and most probably determining, influence of the Reverend Charles Wadsworth, one of the leading pulpit orators of his day. Again, in what direction and with what fixedness ? All these are immensely important questions for a shy, sensitive, and secluded artist like Emily Dickinson. But how many of them are capable of solution still remains to be seen. Then there is the question of how she would have reacted to the high sensitiveness of most of her serious critics to the fact that she was a "woman"—and her diction, tone, masks and poetic thoughts are, therefore, appropriate only to a woman, not to a man, and they feel ill at ease if a man had to write that poetry.

Questions such as these I leave to biographical critics. My business in the present book is with the "what" and "how" of the imaginative experiences she has created in her poems.

As already remarked, my approach to her poems will be formal and analytical. The structuring of the chapters that follow will be around certain salient themes such as death, nature, love, immortality, and non-conformism.

CHAPTER I

Preoccupation with the fact of death

I

Immortality and God are concyclic with religion, and the idea of immortality is explainable with reference to man's terror of death which has its roots in man's sense of sin. The terror of death is, in turn, patronized, or rather dignified, by religion. An ordinary man—so long as he is not a physician, for whom the belief in the inherent eternal bliss is invariably false; or a philosopher, who is prone to refute certain theological assumptions by his purely intellectual preceptions as Toynbee and Russell do[1]—lives in a constant awareness that "in the midst of life we are in death."[2] His effort, all through life, is to achieve that sublime spiritual height which will enable him receive death most serenely and gracefully.

People differ invariably in their guesses as to the sequel of death. For some, the only sequel of death is total annihi-

---

[1]"I am not a believer in a personal immortality; I do not believe that death is followed by." (But Toynbee also admits that he wishes to be free from all of his sins before death undertakes him.) See Arnold Toynbee, "Epilogue," *Man's Concern With Death*, eds. Toynbee *et al* (London: Hobber and Stoughton, 1968), p. 260.

"I believe that when I die I shall rot, and nothing of my ego will survive. I am not young, and I love life. But I should scorn to shiver with terror at the thought of annihilation." Happiness is nonetheless the true happiness because it must come to an end, nor do thought and love lose their value because they are not everlasting. "—Bertrand, Russell, "What I Believe" from his *Why I am Not a Christian* (London, George Allen & Unwin Ltd., 1957), p. 39. (This from fifth impression, 1965).

[2]The prayer for the burial of the dead in the Book of Common Prayer of the Episcopalian Church of England.

lation; the idea fills one with consternation. For others, it is a configuration with the Ultimate Reality behind the visible world. This notion has made it possible for the emergence of the idea of a separate identity for the individual soul against the omnipotence of death. The rest believe that the individual's immortality is the natural sequel of death. The beliefs differ widely, though the wish to maintain a spiritual health until the time of departing from this world is common among the holders of different beliefs.

Each of us has some sense of sin, though one may not be very particular about it. Man's general concern with death is instilled deeply into his sense of sin, in spite of the fact that the key to the relation of life with death is one's familiarity with death and the age at which one became familiar with it.

Emily Dickinson's first experience of death came in April 1844, when at the age of thirteen she witnessed the death of one of her friends whom she admired and liked greatly. Not two years were past when she recorded this shuddering impression in a letter to Abiah Root. The impression she records so vividly and in such great detail that it seems fantastic for a fourteen year old.

The greatest influence on her response to death was the death of her first preceptor, Benjamin Franklin Newton, who was a pioneer in introducing Emily Dickinson to the contemporary British and American writers. He made Emily Dickinson conscious of her latent artistic talents. She has referred to him as a friend who taught her immortality.[3] In a life where sequestration had become a

---

[3]Here perhaps it is for the first time that she uses this word (Immortality) seriously and deliberately. For her "a friend without corporeal frame means Immortality." It seems that after Newton's death, his non-corporeal existence had become all the more meaningful and significant for her. Her gentle talents were invigorated by Newton which later on took the shape of intellectual independence. Newton's help in fashioning her quaint artistic sensitivity was something which never suffered a phase of decline or diminish even at the prime of her poetic genius, and for once (not later than 1862) she realized that those impressions were immortal for her, as far as her artistic personality was concerned. In summer 1862, she wrote to Higginson: "Your letter gave no Drunkenness because I tasted Rum before.... My dying Tutor told me that

deliberately adopted pattern, the deaths of friends and near and dear ones were naturally the main events.[4] A few close ones died in the last few years of her life, and she could not remain stolid to these deaths. She wrote to her cousin in 1883: "The crisis of the sorrow of so many years is that tires me."

To quote C.J. Jung, "One has to be close to death to acquire the necessary freedom to talk about it."[5] It is beyond doubt that the conditions of Emily's life worked to effect a change in her attitude to death. As to what changes or influences her experiences of death brought about in her, cannot be said with any degree of certainty. She witnessed several deaths, but in her poetry she never dealt with them in terms of factual events. So relationships established between her experiences of death and her poetry will amount to no more than secondhand information and, therefore, conjectural and inconclusive. One can, however, say that her concern with death was partly gained by *reflection* and partly by *experience*. Her experiences of death added accuracy to her reflections on death. The deaths of her friends and relatives definitely helped her shape, revise, and confirm her views on a life after death.

Emily Dickinson will be found most rewarding if we focus attention on what her imagination has created rather

---

he would like to live till I had been a poet but Death was much of Mob as I could master—then." The tone here has got some tinge of protest to death.

Immortality for her means the continuity of nonbodily phenomenon of life, brain or soul.

[4]Father June 16, 1874;
Mother Nov. 14, 1882;
Gilbert, Oct. 5, 1883;
Samuel Bowles Jan. 16, 1878;
Wadsworth April 1, 1882;
Judge Lord March 13, 1884;
Helen Hunt August 4, 1885;
Josiah Holland Oct. 12, 1881.

[5]C.D. Jung, *Memories, Dreams, Reflections.* (Collin; The Fontana Library, 1972).

than what the event was. As a lyric poet, she speaks in many voices to express different moods and thereby create an imaginative experience. She dramatizes an emotion in terms of a concrete situation.

The deaths witnessed by Emily Dickinson might have stimulated her to write abundantly on the subject, but, ultimately, her concern with death was not intellectual or conceptual; it was neither extensive nor philosophic. It was, basically, poetic. To a philosopher death is an abstract idea, which the philosophic mind is trying to pierce. Philosophers touch on the problems of death from a conceptual point of view. Schopenhauer, who deals vividly with the problem of death, will serve as an example. He declared that death was the muse of philosophy, notwithstanding that the muse was seldom avowed.[6] Philosophers feed this unavowed muse on such controversial problems as what should be done to mitigate and overcome the fear which death tends to inspire. Among the philosophers there is no controversy on the point that death is something that man is afraid of. They also deal with how man learns about death, or whether death is a natural phenomenon, or what specific psychological or social conditions tend to heighten one's awareness or fear of death.[7]

And then, there is the obvious difference between the poet and the philosopher. The philosophic mind functions on the speculative level of consciousness, and the poetic mind on the visionary level. The poetic imagination constructs all possible models of awareness. At a higher level, the imagination becomes one with the experience it seizes. The imaginative experience sounds as accurate as the gross sensuous experience though its logic is not intellectual, but metaphorical. For a philosopher, the primary realities are intellectual.

---

[6]*The Encyclopedia of Philosophy*, Paul Edwards, ed. in brief (New York; Macmillan Co. and the Free Press, 1967).

[7]As about the problem of fear caused by death, the philosophers can be divided into two main sections. According to some, only the hope of personal immortality reconciles man to the fear of death. According to the others, the fear of death can be mitigated or overcome only when death is accepted as an ultimate end of the individual person.

He deals, in abstract terms, with abstract ideas but, for a poet, those realities are emotional. That is why a poet uses images, objects, and sensations at the level of the imagination to identify the human and the non-human world, and thus create an experience which has a verbal mode of existence.

II

Because I could not stop for Death—
He kindly stopped for me—
The Carriage held but just Ourselves—
And Immortality.

We slowly drove—He knew no haste
And I had put away
My labor and my leisure too,
For His Civility—

We passed the School, where Children strove
At Recess—in the Ring—
We passed the Fields of Gazing Grain
We passed the Setting Sun—

Or rather—He passed Us—
The Dews drew quivering and chill—
For only Gossamer, my Gown—
My Tippet—only Tulle—

We pased before a House that seemed
A Swelling of the Ground—
The Roof was scarcely visible—
The Cornice—in the Ground—

Since then—'tis Centuries—and yet
Feels shorter than the Day
I First surmised the Horses Heads
Where toward Eternity— (J. 712)

"Because I could not stop for death" is a poem surrounded with much commentary. Allen Tate has commented that "if the word 'great' means anything in poetry, this poem is one of the greatest in the English language."[8] His discussion of the poem is a pioneering example of close textual study of thoroughness that the earlier criticism lacks. He has, however, a deterministic approach and omits the fifth stanza of the poem from his discussion. The result is that he finds the poem interfused with "erotic motive." He goes to the extent of declaring it a "love poem" of Emily Dickinson where a lady is courted and ultimately taken away in a coach by a kind gentleman of New England under the shade of death. Tate suggests that she sees, like the nineteenth-century Romantic poets, "love as being a symbol interchangeable with death."

Tate's interpretation of the poem is slightly modified by Richard Chase. Chase, too, finds death to be a gentleman visitor, or lover, and comments that "Immortality in this poem should be the destiny of the Journey and not a passenger of the coach."[9] Chase argues that the gentleman is also God. The theme of the carriage-ride is elaborated by Charles R. Anderson too. Anderson interprets it as a conventional courtship in Emily Dickinson's time. According to Anderson the main theme of the poem is the Journey of celestial marriage. But Anderson's warning here is more important: though the poem at first seems "like another version of the procession to the grave, this is a metaphor that can be probed for deeper levels of meaning, spiritual Journey of a very different sort."[10]

A survey of the teeming body of criticism on the poem underlines the fact that the minds of the critics are somehow or other preoccupied with the ideas of "love" and "marriage." To see the love motive in this poem is not only a false assumption but a treachery against the theme of the poem. Freudian critics of Emily Dickinson sabotage the poem to fit it into their preconceptions and arrive at logi-

---

[8]"New England Culture and Emily Dickinson," in *The Recognition of Emily Dickinson*, pp. 160-161.

[9]Richard Chase, *Emily Dickinson* (New York, 1951), pp. 249-250.

[10]Charles R. Anderson, *Emily Dickinson's Poetry*, pp. 241-246.

cally untenable conclusions. Thus, by reading the poem simply as a love poem, one is very likely to miss the "idea" of the poem, which, though commonplace and ordinary as it seems, constitutes its descriptive level of meaning when viewed in the wider perspective of her unified poetic vision.

If we do away with the load of critical commentary on the poem, we shall find that the poem has four kinds of meaning: descriptive meaning, symbolic meaning, stylistic connotations, and the poetic meaning. Then there is the unification of the experience created by the poem with the theme of death in the total body of her death poetry.

On the descriptive level, the poem deals with the poet's journey with death. The trip is a casual one which the poet accomplishes without any formal preparation, physical or mental: "For only Gossamer, my Gown—/My Tippet—only Tulle—." The six stanzas cover a very long space of time, which is almost endless. The poem begins with a casual stopping of death at the door of the poet and ends with the gate of eternity. In between, the monotony of journey is avoided by a pictorial description of the side scenes in a balanced and penetrating tone.

The poem was composed in 1863, and the title "The Chariot" was given to it by its first publishers. As is usual with Emily Dickinson, the poem has got alternative readings for four lines (9, 10, 20, and 21). The narrator of the poem is a woman who travels with death in a coach which is heading towards eternity. She is a dead person whose post-mortem consciousness, though completely overpowered by death, has the images of memory intact. She is not oblivious of the sensuous experiences and objects (The Dews drew quivering and chill—). As the coach advances one feels that the narrator and the reader are being led to a bond, for the reader internalizes and absorbs the experience. The poem is in the first person, and through the use of common visual images to describe the sideviews of the journey, the narrator illuminates her own identity.[11] The style of the narrator is not high

[11]Narrator's identity is never disclosed as 'he' or 'she' identity. But in lines 15 & 16 the reader is given a vivid description of the narrator's dress, which ensures that the narrator is a lady. 'She' pronoun will be used for the narrator on the same basis.

flown, and the language is not ornate.

On the surface, there is no terror of death. Though the call of death is sudden, there is no overt protest, sense of loneliness, or complaint. There is no fear of the annihilation of life, no sense of doubt, as if she had had some premonition of the incident. Before the journey had had started, the narrator was busy in her domestic chores and "labour,"[12] or activities of "leisure," i.e. the light and serious sides of daily life. But at the time of departure there is no sense of regret, loss, or agony. There is only a sudden withdrawal from the activities of labour and leisure without any complaint against "dark encroachment" of the "old catastrophe."

The opening lines express a sense of confidence on the part of the narrator, a conviction that she is not being taken in a wrong carriage. The tone is apologetic to death, who "kindly stopped" for her, with the implication being that she was supposed to have waited and stopped for death:

> Because I could Not stop for Death—
> He kindly Stopped for me—

The repetition of the word "stop" in the first two lines has the active verbal sense of movement and complete stasis simultaneously To stop clearly means the cessation of movement, but stopping is an activity.

The third and the fourth lines of the poem bring to focus the number and identity of the travellers in the coach. We see a trinity of passengers—the narrator, the coachman (Death), and Immortality. In the third line the expression "but Just Ourselves" suggests the closeness of the narrator with death The "Immortality" of the fourth line is a separate identity. "Ourselves And Immortality," as if "ourselves" is one entity, and Immortality another.

Tate comments that "the terror of death is objectified through this figure of genteel driver, who is made ironically to serve the end of Immortality."[13] Chase also comments to

[12]Labor '—the derivation of the word for this poem may be from Bible, Revelation.

[13]Allen Tate.

the same effect. The first thing I should like to suggest is that the casual tone of the poem leaves no place for "terror" or any other horrifying emotion. Secondly, it is very clearly mentioned that Immortality is not the end of the journey as Chase and Anderson would have us believe, unless they identify Immortality with Eternity. But the phrase "Just ourselves/and Immortality" is a figurative expression for *Just our immortal selves.*

Emily Dickinson's ideas about death are well within the theological framework of Christianity, according to which the soul in human personality is of immortal essence. The statement, "The carriage held but just ourselves/And Immortality" assumes that the journey was actually the journey of the immortal soul. The soul of the narrator had spent a physical life in the mortal body. Death comes to take the soul away from the physical body which had been its home so far. The immortal soul will henceforth be ushered in by death into the world of eternity, very different from the ordinary physical world we know. It is one of the three passengers of the coach. The end of the journey is "eternity," which should not be confused with "Immortality." Emily Dickinson is never careless in her use of these two words; she clearly distinguishes the three terms—eternity, immortality, and the self:

Behind Me—dips eternity—
Before Me—Immortality
Myself—the Term between. (J. 721)

"Eternity" is behind and "Immortality" before, the latter being closer to the poet, though she is considerably aloof from both.

In the poem under discussion "Immortality" is metaphorically a passenger, one part of the bisected self of the narrator: "Mind without corporeal frame" is Emily Dickinson's definition of Immortality. When she talks of herself and Immortality as two separate entities, she means to emphasize that sense of duality or "bisection" which the poet always feels within her. One part of the self is mortal, the other immortal—

though both the parts must go through death to achieve the rebirth into an eternal state of consciousness. Both of these parts are present in the carriage. The indwelling spirit is the immortal part of the narrator. Here the distinction is between the mind and the consciousness of the narrator. Ordinary consciousness is dissolved into death consciousness, and part of the mind is immortal. The poet's recognition of her non-corporeal self in the moments of complete identification with death consciousness is remarkable. Death consciousness is personified as the narrator of the poem. This split within is best illustrated in another poem :

> I felt a Cleaving in my Mind
> As if my Brain had split
> × × × ×
> The thought behind I strove to Join
> unto the thought before— (J. 937)

For a discussion of imagery in the stanzas that follow the opening one, the bisected self of the poet demands some particular attention. The mortal part is concerned with the sense experiences and immortal part with imagination. The first three stanzas deal with the corporeal self's visual experiences, and the last three with the immortal self's imaginative sensations—when the latter becomes free of the laws of time and space.

The introduction of the passengers is succeeded by an immediate movement of the carriage. In the second stanza of the poem the journey takes a slow start. As the coach proceeds one feels that the speaker is going away and further away from the worldly labours and duties—with no feeling of resistance or regret—"We slowly drove—Heknew no haste—". Here the speaker's tone is completely balanced. In the succeeding stanza all of a sudden the movemen tbecomes fast—though the speaker still manages to maintain the sense of identity with the outside world. She can have a clear view of the road as if the coach is a "glass coach." The images of the school children, fields and the setting sun are familiar sights which Emily uses recurrently in so many other death poems.

By an analysis of these three conspicuous images of the poem we can very easily penetrate the mind of the narrator. The images of child, grain and sun are used in a significant manner. They represent, respectively, three progressive stages of life—beginning, prime, and end. In this comprehensive anthology of scenes, the images are very neatly woven. The cardinal points of the poem are marked and moulded by the peculiar pressure on the terms "we passed."

> We passed the School, where Children strove
> At Recess in the Ring
> We passed the Fields of gazing grain—
> We passed the Setting Sun—

Emily Dickinson gives alternate readings for lines 9 and 10 (9: strove/played; 10: Their lessons Scarcely done). "Strove" in line 9 seems more appropriate for two reasons: (a) it does not break the unity of the sound pattern which the other lines maintain ; (b) *School-Strove*—here an imperfect assonance is found in the vowel sound of /o/ and alliteration in the consonant /s/. It produces an effect of concentration of sound. If we adopt "played," the alternate reading for this line adds spontaneity to the poetic meaning. Children are busy in their game and have not finished their studies. But the adopted text seems to be appropriate in view of the poetic device *i.e.* alliteration, which contributes to the lyrical effect of the poem.

The "Setting Sun" comes, in the series, as the last "landmark" in the progressing journey. With it starts the shift in the narrator's consciousness from one world to another. "The Setting Sun" is obviously an emblem of the end of life. The "Sun" symbolizes the wholeness and completeness of life. Another remarkable thing is that the deceased one still does not lose the sensuous perception or the physical identity. There is no clash between the idea of immortality and physical disintegration.

At the climax of the third stanza, the narrator becomes one wave in the current of progressing time. She now shifts from the level of sense perception to that of imagination. The carriage had started with a slow movement, by degrees it became fast, and ultimately the movement reached a point of relativity :

> We passed the Setting Sun
> Or rather—He passed Us—

Both these states represent mortal and immortal self of the poet. The ordinary consciousness of the narrator changes into mythopoeic consciousness. During this process of transformation the smooth running Common Meter of the other stanzas is loosened.

> Or rather—He passed Us—
> The Dews drew quivering and chill

In these lines the loosening of the stanzaic pattern makes the lyric rhythm more precise.

> The Dews drew quivering and Chill—
> For only Gossamer, my Gown—
> My Tippet—only Tulle—

In this stanza subdued horror and some disturbance caused by the act of facing death is suggested by alliteration, assonance and broken stanzaic structure. The word "Chill," intensifies the effect of the cold atmosphere and adds grimness to the situation. And the alliteration of the plosive sounds adds to the grimness from the unconscious level of the mind : *D*ews-*d*rew: *G*ossamer-*G*own; *T*ippet-*T*ulle.

The vivid description of the narrator's dress, which is made of thin, light, and flimsy material, also suggests the perception of cold. In lines 15, 16, the fluid element of casual mood receives a verbal emphasis. While starting her journey, the poet had done no formal preparation. It was for the poet a sort of home coming.

The fifth stanza shows Emily Dickinson's power to fuse in one phrase the entire image of the situation : "A swelling of the Ground—." A pictorial effect is achieved by the word "Swelling." In fact, the whole stanza is rich in visual images :

We paused before a House that Seemed
A Swelling of the Ground—
The Roof was scarcely visible—
The Cornice—in the Ground—

The tone stands in sharp contrast with that in the description of the slow start of the journey—We slowly drove—He knew no haste—. The next three lines suggest the grim atmosphere of the grave. The imagery is radically new. The word "Cornice" in architecture means the uppermost member of the entablature, surmounting the frieze. "A Cornice—in the Ground—" contains an obvious paradox. These lines recall the "low Gate of Eternity" of another poem (J. 303). "In the Ground" of line 20 has an alternative reading, "but a mound." This change, if adopted, will relieve the narrator of the suffocation caused by the "Cornice" which is as low as the "Ground." The "mound" is a boundary fence raised slightly above the level of the earth. But even then the gate remains low.

The last stanza of the poem places the consciousness of the narrator out of time. It passes from the world of three dimensions to that of four. Time is the fourth dimension. The motion of carriage is replaced by motion of consciousness. This motion of consciousness in a particular direction gives rise to a journey which the poet accomplishes through time—i.e. Centuries. Emily becomes rather mystical to conceive the fourth dimension, or gain such an experience as described above :

Since then it is Centuries—and yet
Feels shorter than the Day

Alternate reading in line 21 for "and yet" is "but each." In the first line "it" has been used for "Centuries" and is the subject of the verb "Feels." In the alternative reading "but each" means "but each century". The last two lines of the poem evoke the picture of the horses with their heads turned in the direction of eternity. Eternity is, in effect, a state of human consciousness, though in another poem eternity is a house which has gods at each of its gates.

The most remarkable thing about this poem is that the

idea of personal identity through physical existence does not break down. The narrator can look at the scenery on the way, experience and feel the "chill" of the atmosphere. The third and fourth stanzas are particularly rich in visual imagery.

This poem is an instance of metaphysical conceit as an intellectualized and elaborated single image, that of the bridal journey to describe the funeral procession which is viewed as a journey to eternity. Eternity is only a sensation of consciousness, a mental identification with a physical experience. The narrator of the poem is a discarnate voice speaking from the other side of space and time. The setting of thepoem is deeply religious. The narrator's consciousness assimilates past, present and future into a consciousness which is made of the imagination. The negation of fulfilment is suggested by "And I had put away/my labour and my leisure too...." The tone of the poem is that of a serene acceptance ; the narrator is ready to give up the joys of living and does not mind being dead.

Death is a means through which the narrator communicates with the outer world. This death is not an actual death through which no traveller can communicate : it is an imaginative experience created by the poet. So Death is humanized and behaves like a gentleman. Death is a metaphor, not a theme. Through such metaphors Emily tries to communicate an inner world. To elaborate the metaphorical vision of death, Emily has employed an imagery of which the conceptual implications are Biblical. The following passage from Revelation will explain that the image of death correlated with horses is extracted from Bible :

"And I looked, and beheld a pale horse : and his name that sat on him was Death." (Revelation. 6 : 8) In Revelation four horses come in quick succession ; there is no carriage. And crowns, power, balances, and death, in that order, are accommodated by the horses, each by one. In the poem the carriage is a construction of the imagination ; a trinity of the passengers is on the travel. But it seems as if the poet was unconsciously aware of the four horses, and that is why at the end she writes "the Horses Heads/were toward Eternity."

Whatever may be her motive for reconstructing the Biblical myth, it is certain that this allusion is not accidental. The whole point of the structure of the poem is rooted in the Bible. In the end when everything else has melted into the air the horses' heads are still there, turned Eternity-*waod.* The emotional vision of eternity becomes an imaginative experience of it.

III

I felt a Funeral, in my Brain,
And Mourners to and fro
Kept treading—treading—till it seemed
That Sense was breaking through—

And when they all were seated,
A Service, like a Drum—
Kept beating—beating—till I thought
My Mind was going numb—

And then I heard them lift a Box
And creak across my Soul
With those same Boots of Lead, again,
Then Space—began to toll,

As all the Heavens were a Bell,
And Being, but an Ear,
And I, and Silence, some Strange Race
Wrecked, solitary, here—

And then a Plank in Reason, broke,
And I dropped down, and down—
And hit a World, at every plunge,
And Finished knowing—then— (J. 280)

"I felt a Funeral in my Brain' is another poem employing the post-mortem consciousness of a dead person, though the attention this time is concentrated on the mind of the dead one rather than on her journey. The images of sense in both the poems impinge on the consciousness of the now discarnate narrator. In the one she travels; in the other she stays where she is and it is the poem that travels. The theme of both of the poems is the same—the discarnate mind passing from one world to another.

A paraphrase of the poem tells us that the speaker recalls her apprehension of the funeral service while she lies in her grave. She remembers the activities of the mourners, the beating of the muffled drums, lifting up of the box, and tolling of the bells. But each procedure leaves a defrauding effect on the senses of the narrator and gradually she is lulled to complete insensation where all fresh "knowing" is "finished." What has not ended are the images of memory. By the time the poem reaches its end, all the senses have departed one by one and the discarnate physical speaker's consciousness has become one with death consciousness.

Though the capacity of the discarnate for actual sense perceptions has departed, the poem is rich in sensuous and pictorial images, because of the narrator's ability to recall the mental aspects of sense impressions, which are essential for the making of a poem. The imagination works on the images of memory. For a positive understanding of the mood and tone of the poem, the readers must move along the rhythm of the poem and respond to the sound pattern which the poem employs to reinforce the feeling, induced on the circumference of death consciousness.

The poem is in the past tense, and the narrator is reminiscing a past event which, because of its strong and vigorous appeal, involves the present once again in its essence. The memory seems to be as sharp as the original experience. The poet visualizes herself once again under the same experience.

The word 'funeral' represents a concrete physical image of a post-mortem ceremony, but as it is in the brain, it does not remain merely a ceremony, but becomes a mental desolation, destruction, transport, uneasiness, and transcendence. It expresses on the whole a particutar mental state.

The poem consists of five stanzas—and each stanza is a typical representation of the different psychic states of death consciousness which gradually becomes free of the activities of the senses.

I felt a Funeral, in my Brain
And Mourners to and fro
Kept treading—treading—till it seemed
That sense was breaking through—

In its first phase, i.e. in the beginning of the first stanza, the sense of sight is still lingering around the dead; the dark parade of the mourners is visible to her. But a concentration on the motions of the bereaved ones, who "kept treading—treading," leads the speaker to a sort of trance. In this semiconscious state she feels that the sense of sight is diminishing. She stares at one thing, i.e. the march of the mourners. This is heightened by the repetition of sounds—"treading—treading till it seemed/That Sense was breaking through." "It seemed" means that the visual powers were fading.

In the first stanza the reader is attracted by the elaborate sound patterns, alliteration, and assonance. The repetition of /f/ in "felt/funeral," and of /t/ in "kept treading—treading till it," gives a strong sense of harshness. Then the repetition of long /o/ in "M*ou*rners to and fr*o*" prolongs the mood of languor and sadness. The repetition of /r/ is not soft but harsh: funeral/brain; Mourners/fro; treading/treading; and breaking/through. The fusion of concrete and abstract is the central feature of the imagery of this stanza. "I felt a Funeral in my Brain" is a typical example in which abstract is followed by concrete.

The second stanza reaffirms that the visual structure of the scene is still under the eyes of the speaker. She can see that the march of the mourners is finished and they are being directed towards their seats. The first phase of the narrator's consciousness continues up till the first line of the second stanza. She can behold the seated mourners, when immediately it is replaced by the second phase. The narrator's attention is now on the sound of the drums. In the first stanza the eyes were the most active part of the speaker, now the focus is on the ears:

And when they all were seated,
A Service, like a Drum—
Kept beating—beating—till I thought
My Mind was going numb—

This stanza conveys the sense of the unity of mood. The beat of the drums at even intervals is reinforced by the movement of the third line. The image and music appropriate to the transitional situation are evoked. The narrator's concentration on a single object (dark parade of mourners) had earlier aroused a sense of physical disintegration. Sound, however, is always more penetrating and effective than sight. And so the quiet effect of the drums now makes the narrator feel a specific kind of numbness in her mind. The rhythm of the drums leads her to a consciousness totally free of visual perception. The "kept beating—beating—till I thought" is full of repetition of hard sounds.

The monotone of the drum beats leaves a stupefied effect on the senses of the narrator. The consciousness shifts from one world to another. Beating of the drums may be said to suggest the termination of one world and entry into another. The drum music provides an emotional correlation from the subconscious of the mind. There is harmony of sound and sense in the poem. As far as the mood or the tone of the poem is concerned, the second and the third stanzas are of special importance.

The distinctive pattern of visual imagery of these stanzas is reinforced by the auditory images. In the third line, we have "till I thought" ; earlier we had "...till it Seemed" in the first stanza. "Till it seemed" obviously shows that the speaker is tentative and hesitant in stating the experience. There is no visible proof in support of what she feels. The "seemed" of the first stanza is logically bound to the "sense" which is on the verge of disintegration, though not yet completely broken. The mental process of the just dead soon replaces the perception of external physical action.

The pointed application of "I thought" to the "mind" is in accordance with the requirements of the poem's tone. The rhyming scheme is sometimes inexact (fro/through) and sometimes correct (drum/numb). In the first line of the second stanza, the metrical pattern is loosened in keeping with the transitional mood, which shapes and reshapes itself to make the reckless consciousness communicable.

And then I heard them lift a Box
And Creak across my Soul
With those same Boots of Lead, again,
Then Space—began to toll,

In these lines the uniformity of mood is maintained with great skill. The narrator's consciousness is in a process of change, the outward symptoms of which are found in the repose which the eyes have achieved lately. The sense of sight once abandoned will never be resumed again. Now, the lifting up of the box is not seen but "heard." The quintessence of the stanza is a reassuring focus on ears and sound. The word "Creak" has a sensory and emotive effect here. It produces a sharp, harsh, grating, and crashing sound and echoes the sense too; it gives us a kind of imitative harmony, onomatopoeia ; "creak across my soul." The sound obviously does not appeal to the ears. Its effect is not on the ears any more, but it causes a general mental apprehension of a shattering, tense, and volcanic experience. A sense of unrest, uneasiness, and torture is conveyed. And the lines become the verbal spurt of a wriggling experience. The situation itself is highly tense, and unrelaxed. The speaker's corporeal frame by this time slips very near to complete disconcert. The avalanche of sound, as the word "creak" suggests, is overwhelming for ears. That is why "across my soul" and not across the ears.

In the first line, "And then I heard them lift a Box," the sound and sight are interfused. Then follows a disjunct death consciousness, which engulfs the physical continuity of the speaker and turns her into a fibreless being, a discarnate. The reflective consciousness now confronts naked nothingness. The consciousness proceeds towards a final destination, and "space" stands primarily for the intervening distance. The space has no activity other than being full of the sounds of death. It becomes itself the sound : "Then Space—began to toll.

As all the Heavens were a Bell
And Being, but an Ear,
And I, and Silence, some strange Race
Wrecked, Solitary, here—

The idea of the preceding stanza continues, and the sound of bells and space are brought into relationship. The whole conscious being of the speaker is its own object of contemplation—that is why "being but an ear." The rhythm of this stanza provides a correlation to the fusion of sensation (Heavens were a Bell), and reflection (And Being, but an Ear).

The intensity of the lyric rhythm is achieved through radically new metaphors: "Heavens were a Bell/Being but an Ear; And I and Silence, Some Strange Race/Wrecked Solitary, here." The "being" is now under the radical recognition that it has no way of saving itself on the physical level. There is no certainly of the senses. There is a quest for psychological continuity, the continuity of the consciousness; and secondly a reversed effort not to sink but float in space. The "being" tries hard not to lose existence; that is why it seeks the philosophical equivalent of senses in "brain" or "reason" (as can be seen in the concluding lines).

Another thing which sounds clear in these lines is that the "being" is in a topsyturvy state in which the normal order of things is confusedly reversed. The framework and the physical context of "being" is entirely shattered: "solitary" and "silence" indicate a state where "mourners" and "drums" have no relevance. The word "solitary" indicates the narrator's deprivation of company and society. That is why there is a sense of loss.

The word "silence" seems to be a contradiction of much that is said before in the earlier lines. The consciousness of the narrator, since the very beginning, has been dedicated to the pursuit of making itself free of the irrelevant associations which time and life and space have thrust upon her. The discarnate has attained "silence" and "solitariness." How and to what extent does the poem suggest this meaning can be seen by a close scrutiny of the imagery, vocabulary, and tone. The accumulated effect of these is one of breaking, cracking, disintegration, and destruction. The word "wrecked" in the final stanza suggests complete ruin of the physical and mental life of the narrator. The silence is achieved only through a destruction of sound and sense :

And then a Plank in Reason, broke,
And I dropped down, and down—
And hit a world at every plunge,
And Finished, knowing—then—

The poetic thought gets its logical culmination in this last stanza. Here it is maintained that, contrariwise, it was expedient for the narrator to achieve that state of radical recognition when she had no way of either physical security, or psychological and intellectual integrity and continuity. There has been no effort of the soul to hold on to things carnal; and as the end nears, the floating consciousness almost sinks down. The last stanza is an exploration and, finally, realization of this fact in relation to her quest for imaginative invulnerability. When the whole body is turned to nothingness, her reason is still there. In other words, life after death has still some kind of sense. But this assumption, too, soon becomes inappropriate and reason turns inside out and upside down. The first line "And then a plank in Reason broke" refers back to the locus of the poetic thought, the brain of the narrator.

The capacity of the brain to sustain through the New England death-bed scene has been used in the most calculated manner. And as the last onset, the migrant sensations once again revisit the same locus before that too breaks away finally. Since the funeral was felt in the brain, the state of Reason has been exploited to the full. There has been a breaking and crashing of Reason violently and abruptly. The brain is conceived as a continuous flow or surge of consciousness. It has provided a platform to the consciousness which breaks away from its locus in the end; it becomes discarnate.

Consciousness was itself the *elan vital*, and brain was employed for some special purpose. The whole experience of dying is created through a curiously wrought pattern of sounds. Emily's deliberate art lets the mood take shape at the deepest level of consciousness. It is as though the narrator's corporeal form disappears completely and she becomes one with death. The plunging down and down is the act of being retrieved in the grave. It has an apocalyptic relation with the state of chaos or dissolution which follows ordinary death. In the apocalypse "soul frequently crosses the water or sinks into it at death." Here there is no water, but as the last act, the brain is sinking down and down as the body is lowered in the grave.

This poem concentrates exclusively on the consciousness of the dead, and disintegration of the body and the senses, the is counterbalanced by the continuity of the consciousness. A question may be asked if it is possible for the funeral service to be performed in the brain of the narrator. The following poem will give Emily's answer :

The Brain is Wider than the Sky—
For—put them side by side—
The one the other will contain
With ease—and you—beside—

The Brain is deeper than the sea—
For—hold them—Blue to Blue—
The one the Other will absorb—
As Sponges—Buckets—do—

The Brain is Just the weight of God
For—Heft them—Pound for Pound—
And they will differ—if they do—
As Syllable from Sound— (J. 632)

A doubt may arise as to whether the narrator of the poem is really deceased and is talking in the voice of a ghost. The answer is yes: for the poem is a psychic projection, in metaphorical language, of the loss of the poet's vision of Circumference, having its poetic parallel in the image of death, represented here purely as an adventure of consciousness.

In both the poems discussed above there is echolalia—repetition of sounds and of thematic words. It is not always possible for a person, as Richard Chase[14] has pointed out, to imagine his own death and funeral. But, none the less, for the eyes of the mind, for imagination, everything is possible which is imaginatively conceivable. For imagination, "the plank in reason breaks." The poem starts with "brain" and ends with "reason." The sensitive brain is seen as peculiarly vulnerable to the onslaughts of death. And the mind floats nervously from one world to another, without any final rest or satisfaction—though it reaches a hereafter.

IV

I heard a Fly buzz—when I died—
The Stillness in the room
Was like the Stillness in the Air—
Between the Heaves of Storm—

The Eyes around—had wrung them dry—
And Breaths were gathering firm
For that last Onset—when the King
B witnessed—in the Room—

I willed my Keepsakes—Signed away
What portion of me be
Assignable—and then it was
There interposed a Fly—

With Blue—uncertain stumbling Buzz—
Between the light—and me—
And then the Windows failed—and then
I could not see to see— (J. 465)

The body is worn out and the brain is tired, the whole organism now welcomes death, as it knows that it has "finished knowing." But what saves the dead from sinking in deep frustration is the fact that her brain and consciousness are not under the false impression that they can cut them-

[14]Richard Chase, *Emily Dickinson's Poetry*, pp. 246-248.

selves off from the finite limitations. She very well knows that infinity is an abstract thought, and not a reality. "I heard a fly buzz when I died" continues the same idea and in the end the narrator submits herself entirely to the collapse, beyond which no more physical or mental activities are possible.

"And finished knowing then" ("knowing" being the verbal abstraction of the mental setting) of the previous poem is in tune with "I could not see to see" of the present poem We have the same sensation of dropping into unconsciousness, after a hard struggle with death. In Todd-Higginson editions (Third Series 1896) the poem was published with unwarranted alterations made freely by the editors, their intention being more or less to please the Victorian readers. The syntax of the poem raised a number of problems and difficulties which different editors and critics have tried to solve with their various readings and approaches.

The setting and background of the poem are, again, a death-bed in a room full of the bereaved ones. The relationship between the setting and the speaker is shown in a flash-back—"When the king be witnessed in the room.' The scene is laid not in the present, but it is in the past, although the voice speaks from the present. All the senses, and even the soul, fail to see the light ; they become progressively insensitive : "I could not see to see."

In the present, the narrator can only recall "then I could not see to see—" and give us things in flashback. It is a mental reconstruction of the past experience as recalled from the point of view of the discarnate in the grave. Senses are no more there, only the consciousness is lingering. An explanation is given of how the narrator was led to that state when everything went totally blank and the senses got freed from their normal activities. It is the narrator's reminiscence of the past event that renders the entire situation with vividness. The most striking feature of that situation is the buzz of the fly, which is "blue," "uncertain," and "stumbling." Fly happens to be the dominant factor against which the speaker was struggling. That is why the fly is repeatedly brought into the focus.

The poem starts with the fly, and then follow other images.

A fly intervenes; the scene shuts itself off from the perception of the narrator. The voice we hear in the opening stanza is that of a deceased person. Her obsession with the fly is neither mental nor outwardly, but has religious overtones. The poem begins with a direct presentation of this situation : "I could not see to see." The statement "I heard a fly buzz—when I died—" is followed by a description of the setting. Then the buzz of the fly goes into the background for a while. The primary aim of the poet is to transfer the imagery to an internal level and thus absorb the situation fully.

The atmosphere is marked with profound silence. "Stillness" contrasts with the curiously opposed "Heaves of Storm." The violent commotion of the feelings at the time of departure is compared to a strong outbreak of storm. The serene moments are contrasted with what seemed chaos at the time of dying, the buzz of the fly. The overall tone of the narrator is one of calm composure.

In the first stanza atmosphere is suggested in terms of auditory impressions characterized by battling silence. In the next stanza, the sense experience is conveyed through visual images, brief and simple :

The Eyes around—had wrung them dry—
And Breaths were gathering firm
For that last Onset—when the King
Be witnessed—in the Room—

The elementary apprehension of death on the part of the onlookers is described in terms of their response, which shifts from anguish to reverence for the great moment of passing away. To understand what the King stands for, we have to see what the poem means as a whole. In all probability it stands for Christ (Biblical reference). But Anderson's opinion is that "The king witnessed in his power is physical death, not God."[15] Firm breaths are ready to face the violent assault. The conflict is there, though it is presented very quietly. There is a struggle between the pensive and the joyful moods. The syntax is a bit ambiguous, like the word "King,"

[15]Charles Richard Anderson, *Emily Dickinson's Poetry*, p. 232.

though the reference to the keepsakes and their assignment in the stanza that follows is given to assuage the tension and make the atmosphere homely. It suggests the speaker's concern for worldly things.[16] Gerhard Friedrich's opinion that "the fly is introduced in intimate connection with "my keepsakes" and "what portion of me be assignable" does not sound convincing in the present context.

The "keepsake" and such other images had better be taken to suggest the dying person's preoccupation with her cherished material things no longer of use to her at the departing hour. Fly is introduced in intimate connection with "light", and not the "keepsake." The mind of the narrator is focused on that part of the experience which is related to the fly. By studying the fly the dying person was able to have some premonition of the future, which is keeping with the religious background. The present does not lose its value, though the imagined future also becomes a part of the experienced reality. The two worlds are apprehended from borderline, the dying person's consciousness, which reflects her resilience.

The problems, as raised by Mr. Friedrich about this poem, are—what is the significance of the "buzzing fly" in relation to the dying person and, second, what is the meaning of the double use of "see" in the last line ?[17] The second problem, we have already dealt with. As for the first one, the buzzing of the fly can be studied for the deeper levels of meaning. With the introduction of the fly, other paraphernalia of the setting come into the background and the fly becomes the dominant factor. In its general meaning the fly signifies evil and mischief. Fly was sent by God for the ruin—plague. Here it stands for the ruinous nature of the situation. The inescapable noise produced by the buzz of the fly becomes, first, a visual distraction, and, then, makes the "light" inaccessible. The narrator feels it to be a bad omen : she is not going to have her salvation. Or, damnation is her destiny, she had been a nonconformist.

---

[16]Gerhard Friedrich, "Dickinson's I Heard a Fly Buzz When I Died," *The Explicator*, XIII (April 1965), Item 35

[17]*Ibid.*, Item 35

The blue buzz of the fly is a symbolic expression of the poet's entanglement with damnation. Here Emily Dickinson, a nonconformist, is herself to be viewed, for the moment, as the narrator. Though she longs for salvation, damnation is her destiny. The buzz is characterized as "blue," "uncertain," and "stumbling." All these characteristics help to articulate her sceptical mood. The presence of the fly in this poem has got no extension in reality beyond its symbolic and literary value. The fly attains a symbolic dimension, for it points to the death which hovers over the dying person. It is to be placed in a literary context.

Some strains of draconian imagery linger about the fly's coming and intervening the light ; it contrasts with the light associated with Paradise in apocalyptic imagery. The soul realizes its propinquity to light but fails to reach it. Light has got its peculiar context in Emily Dickinson's own poetry :

> I saw as if my eyes were on
> Another, till a Thing
> And now I know 'twas *Light*, because
> It fitted them, came in. (J. 1039)

The poet is all the time struggling between faith and doubt. Here we find the agnostic's view of death, although the narrator does not follow her line of thought consistently throughout. Despair is the end, which is not surprising since it is a natural outcome of the abandoned belief and the abandoned disbelief. An attempt at a return to belief is made, belief from which she had wilfully alienated. Her ultimate belief has been only in what she had known or imagined. The theme of death again borrows its splendor from some undissolved images, i.e., undissolved in the descriptive meaning. Certain images come to the mind of the narrator ; they come vibrant with meanings drawn from different contexts.

A sort of religious crisis is there in the impending despair throughout the poem. The atmosphere of composure on the one hand and of storm and inner inadequacy on the other go hand in hand. Redemption in this poem is reduced to a personal condition. The atmosphere and tone of the poem is permeated by an awareness of redemption. All the three poems discussed so far deal with some direct experience of death, which is concerned with the direct vision or sensation of death. The situations are almost alike, with some difference in settings. The occasion is the same—the moment of death—though in one poem—death is personified as a gentleman caller, in another it is a mental recognition of the poet's death consciousness ; in the third poem the moment of death is faced against the bewilderment caused by a deep religious crisis—the poet is to be either condemned or saved. Here Emily Dickinson, a nonconformist, may be said herself to be the narrator. Though she longs for salvation, damnation is her predestination—as she was not a devout Christian. And here death gives her a very complex stimulation—a disintegrated system of sights, sounds, and thrills. But if the narrator is to be damned, the rest of mankind is in no better plight.

La Rochefoucauld said that man can no more look directly at death than he can look directly at the sun. A counter argument to this thesis comes from the Stoics and existentialists who maintain that the fear of death may be allayed only by facing it directly. What is true in Emily Dickinson's case cannot be said with any degree of certainty. To sum up, the fear of death can be overcome, if at all, by a conscious perception of it. Moreover, for Emily as a mythopoeic poet, "to look at death is dying." The "I" of the poems has had a mystical experience and presents death in relation to her own existence in "my labor and my leisure too," she imagines the cessation of her world.

It is possible to argue that a mystical perception of death in relation to one's existence in terms of the Christian myth of resurrection is natural for a Christian. When the hu nan mind reaches the limits of the world (the setting sun, sea and the funeral coach) the language which we ordinarily use in order to describe events in the world (and time) has to be stretched. A mythic language is forged when the ordinary language is put under the pressure of imagination. In many poems, the narrator is really deceased ; in others, the tone is that of a person facing death and struggling for life. In yet another group, death is a psychic projection, in metaphorical language, of the loss of the poet's vision of "circumference."

The fact that theme time of death occurs in as many as half of Emily Dickinson's 1775 poems has been pinpointed by the critics with particular emphasis. Emily Dickinson's interest in this theme was not an incidental one, but a carefully organized and articulated interest. Attempts have been made to determine the cause of her interest in death, to show her basic attitude towards death, and to relate it with biographical facts.

Religion is an underlying factor in her deep concern with death. Pressure to convert her into a Christian was exerted from all sides, but she was filled with doubts and anxiety over "salvation." A deep conflict was there between staunch Puritanism and transcendentalism—one threatening with religious insecurities, and the other reassuring momentary relief from them. Neither was acceptable to her. The American Civil War had made the presence of death more real and accurate. Some poems are genuine illustrations of the tensions and doubts generated by religious uncertainties. But poetry was never for her a substitute of religion.

To sum up, any criticism of Emily Dickinson has to face the problem whether we can really find a telos, a definite theory of death behind her poetry on which we can ground and shape our critical reactions and their development. Several critics have tried to establish this telos by an analysis of her life in the light of many miraculous incidents.

The structure of her poems and also the recurrent images they use can serve as the means of unfolding many values and ideas behind her death poetry. These recurrent images embody authentic and permanent standards of the poet. I have related her death poems one with another with a view to understanding her imagery which creates one great net of structural unity. The typical vocabulary of her death poetry consists of "children," "village," "coach," "bridegroom," "dust," "stone," "drum," "sleep image," "purple," and many bridal images. All these symbolize a journey of the imagination to the realm of death. Some of the poems describe a return from and strange experiences of that world.

V

A thematic study of Dickinson's death poetry (thematic in Northrop Frye's[18] as well as in the general sense) reveals her art of representing thought and sentiment in a work of art. All her death poems, taken together, express her vision of human existence and man's ultimate destiny. Taken together, they project a single unified vision attempted by the poet. Like the traditional tales and myths and histories her poems have a strong tendency to stick together and form an encyclopaedic aggregate,[19] especially because of her conventional hymn meter and biblical images. The ethos of her death poetry is powerfully unified and continuous. Every poem is a fresh reconstruction of the same central vision. This tendency expresses her mythopoeic consciousness. In each era the same myths are reconstructed in a new form, with no radical change in the mythos. In her death poems can be marked a gradual development from conceptual statement ("Death, but our rapt attention/To Immortality—") to sensuous tizzy ("I felt a funeral in my brain") when death becomes a physical and mental reality.

Death in her mature poems is a symbol of transcendental consciousness, which, when penetrated by creative sensibility, becomes a mythopoeic consciousness, i.e., consciousness one with the experience. Philosophisings of the transcendentalists are somewhat intellectual. They encounter the objective reality as outsiders, whereas Emily Dickinson's sensibility becomes one with her experience. Her consciousness becomes the death consciousness. This mythopoeic experience is very deep and immediate, and therefore sensuous. So the overall experience of death is, for Emily Dickinson, an adventure of consciousness—and death becomes sometimes a sort of revelation.

Sometimes there is a religious person's attitude in her poems, sometimes a commonman's. Sometimes she is simply playing with the theme, without any seriousness about it. At

---

[18] Northrop Frye, *Anatomy of Criticism* (Princeton, Princeton University Press. 1971), p. 52.

[19] *Ibid.*

other times, she is in a deeply contemplative mood. In this contemplative mood, the emotions experienced range from joy to fear, agony, suffering, grace, resigned attitude, and bravery.

The structure of her poems and the recurrent images they employ serve as a means of unfolding many values and ideas behind her death poetry. She has got an interconnected body of images and ideas underneath her consciousness which her death poetry fishes out in bits and pieces.

A serious attention is demanded by those poems which use her religious uncertainties about salvation and damnation not only as a poetic thought but also as the structural pattern of the poem. Her belief in hell-fire verged on obsession. She believed outrageously in what she was taught in early childhood, and felt wicked when her life could not conform to the maxims of the Sunday School. The harm did introduce a division between the "*conscious reasonable*" personality and "*unconscious infantile personality.*"

Ambiguity can be found in the ideas of death in the Bible. For Paul, the wages of sin is death; (in Genesis also a connection is made between sin and dying.). Emily Dickinson says that the Bible deals with the centre and her business is with the circumference. God, in the Bible, is the centre of everything, whose circumference is nowhere to be demarcated and, if at all, it is this world and human consciousness. Death, in the Bible, is seen as a symbol of the disastrous alienation between man and God because of sin. For Emily Dickinson, the right relationship to the divine being was conceived as gaining eternity in life. She approached the Biblical meaning of death from a positive point of view by trying to glorify life and maintain personal identity.

The point that she does not lose her personal identity can be illustrated with several of her poems. Emily Dickinson never loses her personal identity by accepting an invisible existence beyond the grave and in the afterlife. There is obviously a connection between the brain and consciousness—i.e., once an irreversible damage has been done to the brain cells, empirically there can be no consciousness beyond. She has her doubts about the meaningfulness of disembodied existence.

Biblical myths are found in displaced versions in her poems and the poet has transferred their authority in a specific manner to systematize her own cosmology empirically derived. These images assume a power in her poetry, analogous to the power held by the *ideas* in the poems of the victorian poets of England, and in America in the poems of Emerson, Whitman, and other contemporaries of Emily. Hawthorne also dealt with the theme of death to the verge of obsession, but for him death was a symbol of evil.

Her preoccupation with death is not less even in poems dealing with nature and love. Tate's remark that "her weapon against Death is the entire powerful dumb-show of the puritan theology led by Redemption and Immortality"[20] is somewhat prejudiced. She faces the issue of death in many of its forms, but the "Puritan theology" ultimately does not resolve the question marks which stare her in the face. As a matter of fact, it is Emily Dickinson's reconstruction of the Christian values which saves her in these moments, and not the Puritan theology. At times, of course, we discern in Emily Dickinson the sense of fear and loneliness caused by death which is more or less attributable to her Puritan theology, and the Bible has definitely provided her with patterns and phrases to equip her with the frames and molds in which her personal Christian conception can take form and shape.

Death is for Emily Dickinson (in some of her poems) an obsessing and uncomfortable presence—a "stubborn theme"—though its sooty side is covered up with lively pictures and images which she uses in complete abstraction. Thus she deals with death relentlessly, and one finds it difficult to decide whether her recurrent treatment of this theme is a means of expression or of escape from the fear through an excessive use. We are familiar with her tastes, her readings, her age, her life, and, above all, her religious heritage though she could never identify herself with these things without discomfort. And at this point the evidence is explicit. Emily Dickinson's death poetry is more controversial than either

[20]Allen Tate, Emily Dickinson from *Collected Essays* (Denver : The Swallow Press, 1932). Reprinted in *Twentieth Century Views* on Emily Dickinson edited by Richard B. Sewall.

her love poetry or nature poetry. She thought of death in as many ways as perhaps no other poet has thought of or conceived of so far—but she has never defined or fixed it in any rigid terms.

There can be two broad divisions of her treatment of the theme—death as an event and dying as a process. Death as an event was something from which she learnt wisdom and guidance for her poetry. Death was for her, as I have repeatedly stressed, an adventure of consciousness. That is why to define it in any fixed abstract terms will amount to reducing to abstractions the sum of sensations, thoughts, and feelings which go round and round in circles through the lingering death consciousness of the poet.

There can be, however, four main divisions of the treatment : romantic, philosophical, sentimental, and sensuous. I centered my discussion on the sensuous elements of her poems. The development of her art in treating death is from the objective and imaginative to the sensuous experience of death—when death is no more a side view, but a part of the consciousness. As a matter of fact her attitudes to death are not consistent and orderly. Persuasive and basic contradictions exist in her reaction to the reality of death. There is no definite pattern of the reactions. Her reaction is of the moment, and not fixed. Another reason for this is that as a lyric poet she speaks in manifold voices—male, female, and childlike—to express different moods in regard to the same thing. Her conception of death as an aspect of reality is, therefore, perspectival, and not dogmatic.

Since the maturity of taste in Emily Dickinson's poetry has advanced bit by bit, critics have tried to seek far-fetched relation between the deaths she witnessed from her impressionable years onwards and the death poems which supposedly illustrate the critics' glib speculations. Attention of the critics has also been directed to such minor facts as the imagery of funeral procession in her poems, her use of death as a Puritan (Chase), and so on *ad infinitum*.

As for my own attitude, my study of the poems has used only such historical and biographical data as may help in tacklingthe history of her poetic development, and not in recording the incidentswhich the Amherst girl had in the transaction of her day to day life. As for the fear of death, Spinoza's theory is that the fear of death may be overcome by diverting attention from it. The philosopher's view is that human misery causes painful preoccupation with death. A happy man is not seriously pained by the thought of death, nor does he dwell on the subject. Bertrand Russell is one of the upholders of this view.

Several branches of Christianity theorize that the attainment of total happiness on this earth is just impossible. Christianity also believes that the cure of the fear of death is necessary in order to achieve total happiness in life. Happiness is, therefore, not a cure, but a byproduct of the cure. The knowledge of death gives to life a sense of urgency that it would otherwise lack. The same point has been made by Freud, who compares life without the consciousness of death to a Platonic romance or to a game played without stakes. Heidegger makes a very good point when he says that the awareness of death confers upon man a sense of his own individuality. Dying, he says, is the one thing that no one can do for you, each of us must die alone. To shut out the consciousness of death is, therefore, to refuse one's individuality and to live inauthentically.[21]

Emily Dickinson's preoccupation with death makes her a deeply religious poet. Her imagery in her death poems is drawn mainly from the Bible. We now see "through a riddle" (Paul's remark), "through a glass darkly"—is echoed and reechoed in her death poems.

The Bible proclaims the paradisal vision and talks of living in it perpetually after death. That vision she has had in her encounter with the circumference. But the circle of her cosmology will be incomplete if she does not create the last link of the post-mortal eternity.

This eternity, which is based on the belief that the paradisal vision cannot survive the extinction of the human mind, presupposes death. "Because I could not stop for Death" is a superb example of this vision. Here death is the precursor of eternity. The world which the Bible prescribes for her is

[21]Quoted in Arnold Toynbee, *Man's Concern with Death*, Epilogue.

one of a promised Eden after death—an Eden in which she will live eternally. There are assumptions of salvation and redemption related to it. At times we find in her the fear of loneliness of death which is more or less attributable to her Puritan theology, and the Bible has definitely provided her with patterns and phrases, to equip her with the frames and molds in which her personal Christian conceptions can take form and shape. In fact, the images in her death poetry are so homely and familiar that they never carry any melodramatic touch with them.

To sum up, death is a metaphor as well as a fact to express the degree and vitality of that experience which she is going through as a person—and for the poetic self of Emily Dickinson, death is an eternal reality, abiding in the heaven of human imagination in so many forms :

(1) Death as such—objective truth—philosophic and sentimental statements,
(2) Death—as it deprives you of some one—then the narrator is a bereaved person.
(3) Death personified—majestic and dignified; bridegroom images, etc.
(4) Death in terms of the problem of the afterworld—religious crisis and death.
(5) Death in terms of "I", the radical of presentation—to imagine one's own discarnate existence. Here the language and poetic idea both become quite mythical—and it is at this level that death becomes an adventure of consciousness—since bodily it may not be possible for someone to witness one's own death. Death in terms of 'I' is sometimes an objective reality, and other times a sensuous experience.

The philosophic and empiric preoccupation, which the death poems reflect, the subtleties with which they delight, and the many statements which they employ, remove them from the realm of traditional death poetry. Sometimes they are metaphysical statements about death rather than imagistic poems. The theme of death is surrounded by the idea of immortality and eternity. Death provides the enveloping cover under which, by the creative act of her Muse, she slowly organizes the death world of her own.

If we place Emily's treatment of death in the American tradition, we shall find that she has a close affinity with the Puritan view in a broad sense. She has affinities, for example, with the seventeenth-century American metaphysical poet Edward Taylor, a Puritan Priest, who looks upon death as a mode of assessing man's life in its entirety, life here and life hereafter. She is closer to Taylor in her view of death than to any other poet on the theme, American or English. And yet she knew nothing about Taylor's poetry or his treatment of death. Though her poems on death bristle with theological implications, as illustrated by the poems analyzed, I prize her achievement greater in the poems which create the experience of dying first, and then riddle the experience with theological implications.

CHAPTER II

Treatment of Nature

Nature and God—I neither knew
Yet Both so well knew me
They startled, like Executors
Of My identity.

Yet Neither told—that I could learn—
My Secret as secure
As Herschel's private interest
Or Mercury's affair— (J. 835)

I

If God Emily Dickinson did not know, she declares she did not know nature either. Nature's tangibility as well as its ultimate elusiveness she described, though it always remained a "dissembling Friend" for her. Dickinson's consistent use of the common phenomena of nature suggests her predilection for the known and the familiar as a refuge from the mysterious in life. The images that appeared most frequently in her poetry, after the death images, are, of course, those of bumble bees and butterflies, sunsets, sparrows and spiders, and cycle of seasons, summer being most dear and popular with her.

Emily chose the above mentioned nature images because she knew them intimately. Later in her poetry, the words like awe and despair, immortality and heaven, become, as familiar as the birds and the rainbows. Even then, the world of nature she knew best expressed her profoundest thoughts. It should not surprise any sensitive critic of Emily Dickinson's poetry, therefore, if a universally acknowledged poem, on as important a theme as Immortality—"Safe in their Alabaster Chambers" —is interpreted as a nature poem, primarily and appropriately. The poem will get a unique sense of proportion if the nature images used there are discerned and understood properly.

Safe in their Alabaster Chambers—
Untouched by Morning
And untouched by Noon—
Sleep the meek members of the Resurrection—
Rafter of satin,
And Roof of stone.

Light laughs the breeze
In her Castle above them—
Babbles the Bee in a stolid Ear,
Pipe the Sweet Birds in ignorant cadence—
Ah, what sagacity perished here !

Version of 1859

Safe in their Alabaster Chambers—
Untouched by Morning –
And untouched by Noon—
Lie the meek members of the Resurrection—
Rafter of Satin—and Roof of Stone !
Grand go the Years—in the Crescent—above them—
Worlds scoop their Arcs—
And Firmaments—row—
Diadems—drop—and Doges—surrender—
Soundless as dots—on a Disc of Snow—

Version of 1861
(J. 216)

Before we start a discussion of the poem, it is very important to know the complicated history of the finalization of its text, which T.H. Johnson[1] has so industriously recorded in his variorum edition. He says, and rightly so, that the poem perhaps never reached a final version to the full satisfaction of its maker, though her "cordial visage" remained on it right from 1859, when the poem was originally written, till June 1861, when she sent it to Samuel Bowles for publication in

[1]T.H. Johnson, *The Poems of Emily Dickinson*, Vol. I, pp. 151-155.

Springfield Daily Republican, where it appeared anonymously in 1 March 1862 issue, in its original version (with "cadence" changed to "cadences"), under the title, "The Sleeping."

During this period of three years, Emily Dickinson worked and reworked on the poem's second stanza a number of times on her sister-in-law Susan's suggestion. Susan never approved of any of the versions of the second stanza which Emily sent to her. On getting a new attempt of Emily on the second stanza, Susan wrote to Emily that "the first verse is complete in itself (and) it needs no other, and can't be coupled—strange things always go alone—as there is only one Gabriel and one Sun—you never made a peer for that verse. . . ."[2] On getting this reply from Susan, Emily once again worked on it, and gave two "variant trial substitutes." She again sent her trial to Sue and asked if the verse was "frostier." There is no record of Sue's answer after this. Perhaps she had already given her final word.

Another important thing about the poem is that this was one of the four poems Emily Dickinson had sent to T.W. Higginson for a critical assessment when she first started her correspondence with him. In *Springfield Daily Republican* the poem was published in its original draft of 1859, whereas to Higginson she sent the second version with a changed line arrangement. There is no trace that Higginson made any special comment about the poem. We do not know for sure what Emily Dickinson finally thought of the poem. There is no other copy in any version or arrangement.

In 1890 T.W. Higginson used the original 1859 version of the poem for some article to the *Christian Union*. Higginson does not at all alter the text, except that he arranges it as two quatrains. For publication, Higginson uses the original version without a title, as Emily Dickinson had left it fair and in a packet (No. 3). Higginson's comment on the poem is :

> "This is the form in which she finally left these lines, but as she sent them to me, years ago, the following took the place of the second verse, and it seems to me that, with all

---

[2] *Ibid.*

its too daring condensation, it strikes a note too fine to be lost."[3]

He then quotes the var nt reading of the second stanza which Emily Dickinson had sent to him originally.

This long account of the finalization of the text is not without meaning. The point is that the criticism of the poem starts with the poet herself, who turns out to be the first perceptive critic of it. And that is why for my interpretation I shall be adopting the text of the original version (1859) for both the stanzas. That was Emily Dickinson's final choice, if at all. Johnson also adopts the same version as final. Suddenly, we see Emily Dickinson as a very conscious poet struggling hard to attain excellence and perfection in her art—and so much self-assured that she respects her art more than the opinion of her advisers.

Susan's comment about the poem is equally intelligent and impressionistic—"I always go to the fire and get warm after thinking of it, but I never *can* again..."[4] Then, Emily Dickinson's "preceptor" Higginson too could not remain immune to the artistic appeal of the poem. It took him good twenty eight years (1862-1890) to discover that his reaction to the poem was favourable—a "condensation too fine to be lost."

After Higginson a host of critics have written on this poem, mostly in eulogizing terms, which it rightly deserves. The critical commentaries of William Howard,[5] T.H. Johnson,[6] Charles R. Anderson[7] are detailed and intensive, which take into account all structural niceties and unusual patterns of the imagery with searching critical acumen. Besides, almost all published scholars on Dickinson, so far, have made a passing comment on it, though much could

---

[3]T.W. Higginson, *Christian Union*, XLII (25th September, 1890), p. 393.

[4]Susan's reaction to the second stanza.

[5]William Howard. "Dickinson's Safe in Their Alabaster Chambers," *The Explicator*, SVII (June 1959), Item 62.

[6]T.H. Johnson, *Emily Dickinson : An Interpretive Biography* (Cambridge, Mass : The Belknap Press of Harvard University, 1955), pp. 106-108.

[7]Charles R. Anderson, *Emily Dickinson's Poetry: Stairway of Surprise*, pp. 269-75.

have been expected of the ones who had avowed at the outset of their critical studies to pay special attention to her symbols, metaphors and imagery. It comes to me as a shock that Indernath Kher should have dismissed it as a minor poem, after talking about it so frugally in a few words : "The Alabaster Chambers seem safe, and death provides a "Rafter Satin."[8]

I can safely say, without sounding too presumptuous, that this is one of those few poems which are written in a characteristic Dickinson style, so distinct from any other poet's because of its metaphor, set of images, theme and meter, that here the poet cannot be *known* from the poem, as one cannot know the "dancer from the dance."

Johnson, Anderson and other serious readers of this poem have all unmistakably taken it to be a fine specimen of Emily Dickinson's death poetry, which ends by inviting rapt attention to the theme of immortality.

It cannot be challenged that the presence of Emily Dickinson's dearest theme, death, is vital and easily discernible in the poem; and yet it is definitely neither a death poem, nor one dealing singularly with the idea of immortality. The sleeping "meek members of Resurrection" are there, safe and secluded, unaffected by the revolution of the day, they are not of central importance to the overall imagery of the poem which is so fluid, fresh, and neatly fitted into its structure, that you take out the "Morning", "Noon", and "Sun"; upset the images of "breeze", "Bees" and "Birds"; put out of order the "Crescent", "Firmaments" and "Soundless" dots "on a Disc of Snow," the members of Resurrection, i.e., the departed sousl, placed so serenely and placidly otherwise, will be shunted into the yards of unnoticeability.

The theme of this poem is so mercurial that the best thing to do is not to name it or compartmentalize it strictly on that basis. That is why I do not at all mean to say that it is exclusively a poem of nature either. Johnson has, however, touched on these ideas, as he ends his comments on it by adding that "the reader is suddenly conscious that the motion of the second stanza has become gently rhythmical, as though

[8]Indernath Kher, *The Landscape of Absence*, p. 192.

a cosmic Mother Nature were rocking her children, now suddenly asleep."[9]

My choice of this poem in this particular chapter is conscious and deliberate. For a poem, to which the poet avoided giving any title, in spite of her sustained and unfailing effort and skill to make it nearly perfect artistically, and which was published under an arbitrarily given title "The Sleeping" by its first publisher, who can say with certainty it is either a death poem or a nature poem, or both, or none of the two! We will in fact be more kind to it if we could shift our attention from its theme and examine its form and structural components first, and then see if the pattern of images warrants the presence of any theme assuringly.

Dickinson presents a few images, independent and having a very broad spectrum, from which a background setting springs. "Alabaster" and "Snow" —these two belong to Emily's spectroscopic band of images from nature which occur in much of her writing. And here, they stand for the discoloured and obliterated remains of life. "White as alabaster" she uses in one of her letters as a symbol of death. "Snow" and "alabaster" are used here to convey the same idea, the sense of hardening into death. The snow that takes away the life of the season is referred to by her as the "Alabaster Wool" in another poem. The setting of the present poem from the very beginning is controlled and well chiselled. The "meek members"—meek because the discarnate are in perfect repose, are lying down in the world of imaginative faith and unity. They do not have to struggle either in mind or through the senses for their elemental or psychological sustenance.

They are "safe," since there is no danger of being decreed by mortal destruction. The word "safe" gives rise to a muted, affirmed, and austere situation. Then there is a perfect liaison, a harmony with nature. The forward movement of time which is living and growing, does not affect the slumber of the souls waiting for resurrection. In the fifth and the sixth lines —"Rafter of Satin And Roof of Stone"— the scene and

[9]T.H. Johnson, *Ibid.*

the idea are firmly grasped by the radiant, clear, dazzling, and sharp images. The image of Stone, symbol of hardness and nonchalance, fills the atmosphere with the sense of the emptiness of inanimate nature—and makes the subsequent soft and bubbling nature images more precise and enduring in their effect by serving the point of contrast.

In the subsequent stanza, one finds the music, poetry, and landscape of the imagination blended together. The poet sets the scene (breeze, castle, Bee, Piping Birds), and also lists the sounds—laughing of breeze, babbling of Bees, and "ignorant cadence" of birds. All these images come intuitively and instinctively, and they seem to project the emotion quietly. And yet it appears that the senses are not enough. The whole idea has been conceived in the eye, ear, and also mind—"Ah, what sagacity perished here !" And, there the stanza ends. The Puritan theology looks upon nature as "an apparent evil within God's larger plan,"[10] but Emily presents it as gentle, sweet, sincere, and grand.

At first sight, the poem under discussion seems to be of the overt nature, rather than of the inner nature of man's mind, but in the third stanza, where the speaker's voice becomes more eloquent, the images begin to be encircled around the abyss of time, and consciousness seems to be expanding to cover the whole cosmos, (images of Arcs, Crescent and Firmament). "Crescent" stands for the outer edge or curve of the universe. "Worlds scoop thin Arcs" perhaps stands for solar bodies, and "Grand go the Years" clearly suggests the flux of time. "Row" is another archaic term which makes the poetic meaning a bit obscure. "Row" is actually a verb which means to cast light downwards. In the last two lines, "Diadems – drop—and Doges Surrender/Soundless as dots—on a Disc of Snow--," the poem achieves a formal and linguistic self-sufficiency.

The poem starts with the "Alabaster Chambers" and ends with "Disc of Snow." Both the images, combined together, lend a sense of soundness to the poem, and the line,

---

[10]Jean McClure Mudge, *Emily Dickinson and the Image of Home* (Amherst, the University of Massachussetts Press, 1975), p. 161.

as a movement of "time," becomes circular. "Diadems—drop —and Doges—Surrender" has four pauses and the reader gets ample time to absorb the whole image mentally. The image suggests royalty—but through a metaphor, not directly. Diadem is the badge of royalty worn on the head—and the doge is a rating dignitary. The words "drop" and "surrender" literally mean the surrender of splendour and glamour in life. Light chuckle of the breeze, the hum of the bees, and sweet cadence of birds all produce a marked contrast to "diadems" and "doges." "Drops" and "surrender" suggest that the end of all the big and glamorous objects is soundless and sudden, unnoticed even by Time: "Grand go the Years" (which watches it very coldly and objectively) "as dots—on a Disc of Snow."

Anderson comments that the "ecstasy of life on this earth is rendered in the banal language of popular literature, the poetry of gift books: laughing breeze, piping birds, and babbling bees."[11] I would, however, suggest that these images are used as the device of paradox to enhance the effect of the poetic meaning. On the one hand, the members waiting for resurrection are lying in their Alabaster Chambers—in a state of total insensitivity—"stolid Ear"—and want of movement. On the other hand, the paradox of the situation is that the world of nature continues—with ease, grace, and liveliness, as ever before. All the nature images are personified—the breeze is in her Castle—laughing at the "pathetic" state of people aspiring to become alive again. Bees babble in their Ears, even if they know that their senses are not receptive now. Piping birds are busy with their songs, even if no soul is there to clap its hands and ask them to sing more. Part of the existence is mortal and part immortal. The situation represented here through lively and appropriate images lends authenticity to them. The immortal part of existence is obviously the world of nature.

The images of nature, as used in this poem, are appropriate in another way too—they add a sense of proportion to the poet's obsession with decay and death. Nature images,

[11]Anderson, *Ibid.*

set against the theme of this poem, suggest the poet's predilection for the known and familiar as an escape from the mysterious in life. Death and immortality are, after all, two of life's incomprehensible and, therefore, terrifying forces. Some most favorite and popular images in Emily Dickinson's poetry are drawn from the world of nature. In one of the poems of her young age she pictures herself as the "little Tippler" :

> Inebriate of Air—am I—
> and Debauchee of Dew—
> Reeling—thro endless summer days—
> From inns of Molten Blue— (J. 214)

II

As a nature poet, whatever Emily Dickinson has written is in keeping with the little tipplers's image of her. A good deal of her nature poetry is just a simple appreciation of Mother Nature with all her little creatures. Some of her finest poems are nature poems only, and they reflect a very sensitive understanding of the mysterious relationship between man and nature. She had an excellent sense of appreciation for the beauty and variety of the natural phenomenon, with all its subtleties and moods.

Around 1860 nature as a theme was favorite with poets, both in England and America. The line had continued from Blake and Wordsworth to William Cullen Bryant and Emerson. This theme has been treated with variety and versatility. For Wordsworth, nature was a moral teacher, a cure of the evils of civilization, an expression of the Divine will, an embodiment of beauty, and a means of glimpsing immortality. There were indeed other poets also who shared with Wordsworth this approach to nature. Among the American poets, Emerson comes closest to Wordsworth. Most of these poets had philosophical ideas about nature. That is why nature as a literary subject soon became stylized.

In this literary context Emily Dickinson's nature poetry has freshness. She, as a poet, never philosophises or idealises nature. She is sceptical of her understanding of nature, and goes on defining it in various ways, without actually reaching any conclusion:

"Nature" is what we see—
The Hill—the Afternoon—
Squirrel—Eclipse—the Bumble bee—
Nay—Nature is Heaven—
Nature is what we hear—
The Bobolink—the Sea—
Thunder - the Cricket—
Nay—Nature is Harmony—
Nature is what we know—
Yet have no art to say—
So impotent Our Wisdom is
To her Simplicity. (J. 668)

The poem represents moods and attitude to nature, popular with Emily Dickinson. First, we have the visual images of nature—abstract and concrete—hill, squirrel, bumble bee, Afternoon, and Eclipse. Then, we have association of sound with images—bobolink, cricket, Thunder, and Sea. And in the end, we have Dickinson trying to arrive at a conclusion by a negative process, and immediately repudiating it and leaving the problem with a few revealing insights but without resolving the doubts. She wants to tell the truth in slant; she tries to solve the mysteries by a negative process—by saying what they are not, than by showing what they are. But her definition that "nature is harmony—what we know—" is quite comprehensive and well concluded. Though the poet is still not sure and admits that she has "no art to say" what exactly nature means to her.

Or, she will express her relative understanding of the relationship between man and nature, basing it on her observations and interpretations. Even in such cases the background and conclusions will be provided by her perennial concerns which we have already termed as "Awe," "Circumference" and "Centre." Her observations are so sharp, precise, and analytical that they themselves become experiences, directly felt by the poet. And the logic of creativity as it is, direct experience expressed in the language of metaphor becomes a vision of it—and then poetry travels from the realm of mental perception to that of mythopoeic consciousness.

Perception, then, becomes more and more centralized, and the consciousness of the poet becomes the circumference which surrounds nature. During these moments of oneness with nature, the poet writes in various moods and wears various masks. Most of her nature poetry is written as what one may call, a kind of direct statement or epigrammatic wit, sharpened by visual pictorial images.

III

A Route of Evanescence
With a revolving Wheel—
A Resonance of Emerald—
A Rush of Cochineal—

And every Blossom on the Bush
Adjusts it's tumbled Head—
The mail from Tunis, probably,
An easy Morning's Ride— (J. 1463)

In one of her letters Emily Dickinson identified a poem by the title "A Humming—Bird." Thisp oem, because of its precise and most unusual description of the bird, has attained a great deal of critical attention. Critics while commenting on this poem have found it necessary to compare it with an earlier poem on the humming bird. The earlier poem (J. 500)*, written some twenty years before the second one, is much more direct, discursive, and longer; still there is some point in comparison.

---

*Within by Garden, rides a Bird
Upon a single Wheel—
Whose spokes a dizzy Music make
As 'twere atravelling Mill—

(*contd. on next page*)

In the earlier poem, the humming bird's abode is the poet's garden and apart from the revolving wheels and the flowers, and a feeling of nostalgia at the vanishing sight of the humming bird, the poet is in the company of her dog, and not alone.

The second poem is more precise, has economy of expression, and is penetrating in its images. This poem is so condensed in its diction and imagery that to find its match in the whole range of English language is not easy. In the earlier poem, the idea of a "Garden in the brain" is there, though it is actually the garden outside which is the setting of the poem, In the second poem, the mind or more truly the consciousness of the poet becomes the garden, and the humming bird is an image therein.

At its literal level, the poem is very simple; it describes a humming bird in movement. The poem presents the vast space—with a humming bird, blossoms, and the narrator. Things are presented as "sensations" through a language in which each word contains a life-size image. Thus we can say that the whole poem is one udified dynamic image.

He never stops, but slackens
Above the Ripest Rose—
Partakes without alighting
And praises as he goes,

Till every spice is tasted—
And then his Fairy Gig
Reels in remoter atmospheres—
And I rejoin my Dog,

And He and I, perplex us
If positive,'twere we—
Or bore the Garden in the Brain
This Curiosity—

But He, the best Logician,
Refers my clumsy eye—
To just vibrating Blossoms :
An Exquisite Reply : (J. 500)

To put it in very simple and easily comprehensible terms, let us imagine a picture—or a picture in movement. If we can keep up imaginatively with the movement of the picture, we will be left out with "place" instead of "presence," like the "Blossoms on the Bush." An evanescent object—or an object fleeting on its way—the speed is so much that it appears like a wheel, moving at great speed. The speed gives rise to a certain sonority, a resounding vibration—which is interwined with the "Impression" of a highly-esteemed gem-stone of green colour. A description of the humming bird's colour is there. Along with emerald and sonority, another preponderous image is introduced, that of cochineal, a scarlet dye-stuff consisting of dried bodies of a Coccus insect gathered from a cactus in Mexico, or in West Indies. Tihe word "cochineal" may stand here either for the insect tself or for the scarlet color.

This picture is neither on the earth, nor in the sky. It is somewhere in between. Then there is a garden with very sensitive "Blossoms." We only see them after the first phase of the movement ofthe picture is over—*i.e.* after the "Rush of Cochineal," adjusting with their loss. The factual statement of the event will be like this: flowers have their petals disturbed owing to the hovering and darting of the humming bird.Then the third and last dimension of the picture—the poetic persona in the background with an amazing sense of surprise and loss of a vision. No sooner is the picture created than it disappears.

It appears that the poet already had a whole picture in the mind—and she just depicted it through very well chosen words carrying images of speed and vanishing—each word containing one full image. In the end, the essence of the poetic idea remains as elusive and transient as the wheeling speed of the humming bird. In the last two lines there is a change of imagery through the metaphors of "mail"—which gives a new dimension to the meaning of the poem. Thus the concluding lines provide a very playful irony—perhaps to give some warmth against the defrosting effect of the poem. Grover Smith gives a very sound interpretation and a new meaning to the poem : "A train travels upon a "route," it is borne along by many a "revolving wheel," its sound is a "resonance" and a "rush," and on it people "ride." These words thus have a double value : they remind us that like the humming-bird itself, a railway train gives a look at the far places of the earth—for those who journey with it."[12]

This poem uses an "aureate diction." That means, the poem is written in big, bombastic, and bumbling words, and each word carries a whole idea, an image absorbed into it. To get the essence of the poem, all that the reader has to do is to open, and bring to life and size each image and picture contained in it. The "meaning of the poem" enters into the scenery painted—small in area, but having the "God's plenty" in its circumference. The picture not only has flat images of a few objects, it has some dazzling and bright colors, some "dizzy Music" caused by the revolving wheel.

All the senses are being called to attention simultaneously—along with the mind which has to cope up with the speed and impressions. Then, the bird's departure is not at all mentioned. It is to be taken for granted to have occurred between the movement and the emotions of the Blossoms with "tumbled Heads." The pictorial element attains the peak of its force in the first four lines. The concluding four lines of the poem are charged with emotional intensity—an after-effect of parting, a sense of emptiness, and that is all. The emotions, too, are jumbled up—a sense of loss, wonder mixed with "Awe", and then the courage to adjust with the loss. The spectator of the whole scenes, gains her poise and the senses are back. But the mental condition can be understood by the "whimsical comment" made at the end.

IV

To understand more exactly Emily Dickinson's originality as a poet, and her capacity to create a deep sensation out of a few penetrating images, we can compare this poem with another poem on the same subject—that is, D.H. Lawrence's

---

[12]Grover Smith, Dickinson's "A Route of Evanescence," *The Explicator* VII (May, 1949), Item 54.

poem on "humming-bird":

I can imagine, in some other world
Primeval-dumb, far back
In that most awful stillness, that only gasped and hummed,
Humming-birds raced down the avenues.

Before anything had a soul,
While life was a heave of Matter, half inanimate,
This little bit chipped off in brilliance
And went whizzing through the slow, vast, succulent stems.

I believe there were no flowers then,
In the world where humming-bird flashed ahead of creation.
I believe he pierced the slow vegetable veins with his long beak.
Probably he was big
As mosses, and little lizards, they say, were once big.
Probably he was a Jabbing, terrifying monster.
We look at him through the wrong end of the long telescope of time,
Luckily for us.[13]

Lawrence's poem gets the essence of the spirit of the bird—that means—the poet identifies himself with the indwelling spirit within the bird. On the contrary, Dickinson identifies the bird with the consciousness in herself—that is why we do not feel a sense of duality between the poet and the object of her narration—both become one, and we only feel the presence of something. The idea of human consciousness becoming one with an object of nature is very abstract, and that is why the images employed to give shape to this idea are very bright (Emerald), concrete (revolving Wheel), and dazzling (A Rush of Cochineal).

D.H. Lawrence's arena of depiction is indeed very big, covering many animate and inanimate cosmic symbols of the

[13] D.H. Lawrence, *Selected Poems*, ed. W.E. Williams, (London: Penguin Books, 1950), p. 105.

natural world as conceived through the poetic sensibility, which seems to be quite mythical here, in the sense in which W.B. Yeats is mythical in his "Sailing to Byzantium." The "other world," "Primeval-dumb," "awful stillness," life as "a heave of Matter," and a world with "no flowers" in it, all these lend a sense of dreamy atmosphere, antiquity, and primitiveness to the poem. Lawrence's humming-bird is viewed through a long "telescope of Time," whereas in Emily Dickinson's case it is just the opposite. The movement of Time is so fast at the moment of "presence" and "place" that the narrator is not able to catch—what is felt is just a deep sense of it.

Lawrence has got "inside the bird's skin"[14]—Dickinson has surrendered her human consciousness to its presence. Again, Lawrence's humming bird has its existence against so many primitive symbols created by the poet—it is present since times immemorial, "ahead of creation," and thus becomes a mythical bird. Dickinson's humming bird is "A route of evanescence," (written in swift iambic trimeter), a soul that has vanished. Lawrence's poetry leaves a strong feeling of sustenance—Dickinson's poem leaves a sense of discontinuity, elusiveness.

This poem is startlingly modern in Emily Dickinson's application of techniques to poetry. Dolores Dyer Lucas has remarked that in this poem "Emily Dickinson's use of language which evokes simultaneously sound, color and motion is a kind of precursor of the modern, popular admonition to mix the media."[15] The humming bird had a very special place in Emily Dickinson's mind. Once while writing to comfort an ailing friend she remarked that humming birds and Orioles were flying by her side when she was writing and she longed to guide their "enchanted feet" to the sick person's chamber.

For another nature poem written in the same state of "transport"—"I taste a liquor never brewed"—most of the critics ascribe its narrator's image to Emily Dickinson—that the "Debauchee of dew," and the "little tippler leaning

---

[14]Northrop Frye, *Fables of Identity*, p. 202

[15]Dolores Dyer Lucas, *Emily Dickinson and Riddle*, p. 124.

against the Sun," is Emily Dickinson herself. But according to one critic, the speaker is not Emily at all. Emerson's remark that air should suffice for the poet's inspiration and he should be tipsy with water, or Thoreau's rhetorical question who does not prefer to be intoxicated by the air he breathes, comes very close to Emily Dickinson's poetic thought in "I taste a liquor never brewed." By the end of the poem the speaker simply declares, "Inebriate of air—am I" and "Debauchee of Dew."

V

On the whole Dickinson's treatment is so varied and attiudes so different that there can be only a few broad categories of her nature poetry. In most of the minor poems, like ther romantic predecessors and transcendental contemporaries he believes that there exists a definite mystical bond between man and nature—

Several of Nature's People
I know, and they know me
I feel for them a transport
Of cordiality— (J. 986)

Once in a letter to her favourite nephew she wrote, "I have borrowed a little honey for Aunt Mattie's cold of a religious Bee who can be relied on." It was in this spirit of delight and mirth that she wrote most of her nature poems, and entered into a bond of friendship with nature :

In the name of the bee
And of the butterfly
And of the breeze, amen !(J. 18)

Nature is not a stern preceptor for Emily, as it is for most of the Puritans. She respects all nature objects as personages of another kingdom, a kingdom significant and symbolic of a high degree of perfection in a higher order of creation. This attitude can of course be found highly objectionable by staunch Puritans. Whatever the seeming perfection and the glory of that "stainless" creation may be, it cannot be pre-eminently superior to its creator. Here she challenges the transcendentalist's attitude and declares that an unbreachable separation exists between man and nature, and that nature is indifferent, and at times superior to mankind.

In a second category of her nature poems can be included those poems which reverse the first attitude, and the feeling of intimacy and oneness with nature gets replaced by a feeling of duality. The most important category of her nature poems is however the one in which her observation of a natural object and her consciousness become one, and she writes like an inspired oracle. T.H. Johnson[15] perceptively remarks that "a distinction can be made between the nature poems that are philosophical and those that are general portraits."[16] Poems like "There's a certain slant of Light," (J. 255) and "Further in Summer than the Birds" (J. 1068); "There is a morn by men unseen" (J. 24), "These are the days when Birds come back—" (J. 130) which express a particular mood of nature along with the poet's reaction to or ideas about it. Such poems are reflective and impressionistic in nature. These reflective poems are mostly written at an early stage of her poetry writing.

What Johnson calls "genre poems" are the ones she wrote at an advanced stage, almost at the fag end of her poetic career. These poems mostly deal with the mystical ideas of the poet, and are very abstract in the use of images, symbols, and metaphors. Her two poems about humming bird discussed earlier are respective representatives of both these phases. It took Emily full twenty years to conceive a garden in the brain.

Some other important poems of this category are "Bring me the sunset in a cup" (J. 128), "I taste a liquor never brewed —" (J. 214), The Wind didn't come from the Orchard—today"—(J. 316), "I'll tell you how the sun rose—" (J. 318), "I started Early—took my Dog—" (J. 520), "A narrow Fellow in the Grass" (J. 986), "At Half past Three, a single Bird"

---

[16]T.H. Johnson, *An Interpretive Biography*, pp. 201-2.

(J. 1084), "It sounded as if the Streets were running" (J. 1397), "As imperceptibly as Grief" (J. 1540), and so on. Emily Dickinson had never aimed to be a systematic nature poet, or to write a complete philosophy of nature—and that is why her poems cannot be made to show a systematic or well developed mode of thinking.

Most of her finer nature poems are written when she is in an oracular mood, "possessed," with "ecstasy," "awe," "wonder" or even "madness." That is why the tone in such poems becomes typically witty, epigrammatic or riddle-like :

A little Madness in the Spring
Is wholesome even for the King, (J. 1333)

"Madness" here is the ecstasy or high mood the poet gets in spring. Her sense of ecstasy in living finds its expression in beauties of nature, and she always remains assured that "exhilaration" is within, "that her whole idea of the outer world takes its shape, size, lustre, color, and flavour from the inner, that the one season she really wants is "midsummer in the mind." She always balances two different presentiments against each other, light against dark, courage against despair, acceptance against longing, and perhaps agrees with Emerson that all things are double, one against another. And this is what gives a dramatic touch to most of her lyrics.

Emily Dickinson's poetry is essentially the poetry of consciousness. Nature is something which is around her and within her. As Emily Dickinson had abandoned a belief in Biblical post-mortal eternity, poetry was the essence which took place of life's redemption. Here Emily Dickinson's attitude is not very much different from Pater's desire of a religion of art, or Santayana's insistence on a greatly enlarg-ed role for poetry and imagination in the place of formal religion. a means by which man could establish the harmony between himself and nature. In such moments of perfect identification with nature, her consciousness becomes the abode of all the nature phenomenon—and characteristically in the nature of an inspired oracle, the poet writes :

"Bring me the sun set in a cup,
Reckon the morning's flagon's up
And say how many Dew,
Tell me how far the morning leaps—
Tell me what time the weaver sleeps
Who spun the breadths of blue !" (J. 128)

VI

The poetry, it seems, is not written. It comes by itself. "How far the morning leaps" or "who spun the breadths" of blue, only an "inspired" person will ask. It is precisely in such moments that the poetic mind becomes oracular, and poetry the "inspired" statement of the oracle. In this mythical phase of her consciousness the "Slant of light" of "winter afternoons" oppresses her "like the heft of Cathedral Tunes." When that mood is over, the poet is left with a "Heavenly Hurt"—and concludes that it is the imperial affliction "sent to her by the air." This other kind of religious experience gained in a state of heightened consciousness is called "transport," or "ecstasy", as Emity Dickinson would like to call it.

Now the poet feels directly in communion with nature; "identity," is another term for it. Nature surrounded by the circumference of "human consciousness," becomes the nature with a "human shape" and meaning, the Eden of Bible. In such moments, Emily Dickinson is frequently overpowered by awe :

It sounded as if the Streets were running
And then—the Streets stood still—
Eclipse—was all we could see at the Windo w
And Awe—was all we could feel.

By and by—the boldest stole out of his Covert
To see if Time was there—
Nature was in an Opal Apron,
Mixing Fresher Air. (J. 1397)

In the "ecstatic" state of mind, the poet visits and revisits lands unknown. This mood ends finally like an end of some vision:

At Half past Seven, Element
Nor implement, be seen
And Place was where the Presence was
Circumference between. (J. 1084)

The images of "Continuous Summer" or noon in Emily Dickinson's poetry symbolize the eternal state of consciousness in harmony with nature. When this vision disappears, at is replaced by ordinary experience. Ordinary experience is lso an ecstatic experience turned inside out:

These are the days when Birds come back—
A very few—a Bird or two—
To take a backward look. (J. 130)

Now, the mind is not a circumference at all, but a centre, and the only circumference is an indifferent and unresponsive nature—"Nature in her monstrous house." Where the mind becomes "Centre" and Nature the "circumference," there is no place for divinity, it has vanished somewhere beyond the sky or beyond life. Some condensed nature poetry Emily Dickinson has written even in this state of consciousness. These "awful" and unsympathetic moods of nature once again give rise to some intense emotional upheaval:

I started Early—Took my Dog—
And visited the Sea—
The Mermaids in the Basement
Came out to look at me—

And Frigates—in the Upper Floor
Extended Hempen Hands—
Presuming Me to be a Mouse—
Aground—upon the Sands—

But no Man moved Me—till the Tide
Went past my simple Shoe—
And past my Apron—and my Belt
And past my Boddice—too—

And made as He would eat me up—
As wholly as a Dew
Upon a Dandelion's Sleeve—
And then—I started—too—

And He—He followed—close behind—
I felt His Silver Heel
Upon my Ankle—Then my Shoes.
Would overflow with Pearl—

Until We met the Solid Town—
No one He seemed to know—
And bowing—with a Mighty look—
At me—The Sea withdrew— (J. 520).

It is written in the second state of mind when the nature is a 'haunted house,' and she encounters it as if she is encountering death. This poem is variously ascribed as a "love poem" (John B. Pickard) and as a "death poem" (David T. Porter). Its theme may be love or death, that is notuery important, but it is surely a "poem of power" as Yvor Winters acknowledges it. The poem's strength lies in the fact that it can accommodate all contradictory interpretations regarding its theme, and at the same time remain superbly dramatic and highly symbolic.

On its literal level, it is apoet's walk by the sea side along with her Dog. The visit is in a very relaxed and holiday mood. While she is standing "Aground upon the sands—the mermaids And the Frigates" come up at the surface to see the persona. The poetic persona here is obviously a female, as a vividdescription.of her dress shows. (We can refer to her as "she."). The poet remains unmoved, and does not get affected by their presence. But after a while, Sea, personified here first as a "Tide" and then as "He" reaches her and tries to overtake the poet slowly, gracefully, gently and by degrees—"simple Shoe," "Apron," "Belt," "Boddice," and so on. So far, the lady is unmoved, and enjoys the dramatic development of the scene.

But as we reach the third stanza, we can feel the terror and the crisis the persona faces—as if the sea will eat her up.

Against the vastness of the Sea, she feels her own smallness, delicacy, and feminine tenderness all the more—"as a Dew/ Upon a Dandelion's Sleeve." This fear and repulsion does not last long. She regains her previous vitality and strength within no time, and she leads herself away from the "monstrous" grip of it. Thus, in the concluding stanzas, the whole situation is reversed : she is retreating from the sea, with her might and vitality, and "He" follows her as if trying to court her. She is successful in resisting his advances—but regards him as cherishable and beautiful, noting its "Silver Heel." Like it had reached her, the Sea withdraws also in degrees—"Upon my Ankle—Then my Shoes." She enjoys the silver water flowing through her body. In line 16 where she asserts "And then—I started—too"—the verb "started" is deliberately ambiguous—suggesting the beginning of her withdrawal, fear, and sudden terror.

Keeping aside all Freudian interpretations of the poem, my only intention has been to show her in a different state of consciousness while facing nature. But here also we can see that the persona remains very strong and determined. The peculiarity of the poem is in the fact that nowhere in the poem does the persona identify herself completely with any of these interpretations. The success of the poem lies in a very rigoros compression.

CHAPTER III

Intimations with the Experience of Love

I

"In a body of poetry devoted to the main concerns of consciousness," observes Albert J. Gelpi, "the principal themes are predictably love, death and immortality : fulfilment, dissolution, and transcendence inextricably entwined."[1] It is indeed an accurate observation that Gelpi has made. Emily Dickinson's commitment to privacy and the inner drama of consciousness is the fundamental principle of her poetry. Her interplay with undefined psychic and spiritual experiences determines her basic subject, which is imagination entangled in the drama of "Centre" and "Circumference."

In Dickinson's poetry, the notion of "Circumference," what we will call now the "duo-consciousness," is used as a springboard for expanding her concepts of death, nature, love, and immortality. This duo-consciousness is something which just happens for no definable or predictable reasons. Under the impact of this consciousness, the poet experiences intense happiness and affirmation. It happened to Blake when he was looking at a grain of sand, and he could see the whole world into it. Duo-consciousness for Emily is like a visit of the heaven—it gives her a feeling of eternity.

In her dealings with "death" as an adventure of consciousness, or during the experience of "dying" as a process of the dissolution of emotions : or even in the mood of total identification with nature, this duo-consciousness, as we have already observed, is experienced in flashes. It is not a permanent state of mind. In her love poetry, Emily tries

[1]Albert J. Gelpi, *Emily Dickinson : the Mind of the Poet*. (Cambridge: Harvard University Press, 1965), p. 109.

to make it more or less constant. An "evanescent vision"—her common metaphor in nature poetry (the same as Allen Tate called "death"—the general symbol of nature)—becomes in love poems a source of perennial struggle, and the poet's ultimate triumph over it. The separation of two lovers on the earth invariably results in their reunion in immortality, as a sequel of "the brief Tragedy of Fresh" (J. 664).

While it is alive
Until Death touches it
While it and I lap one Air
Dwell in one Blood
Under one Sacrament
Show me Division can split or pare—

Love is like Life—merely longer
Love is like Death, during the grave
Love is the Fellow of the Resurrection
Scooping up the Dust and Chanting "Live" ! (J. 491).

In this poem the persona's consciousness becomes like an ancient archaeological sight with layers upon layers of an "sceptical awareness" of non-separation : "*One* Air," "*One* Blood" and "*One* Sacrament." Side by side, there is an area of the mind that is sensitive and alert against the fear of separation—"Oneness" is alive only till "death touches it." In the first part of this poem, the tone is numb and tense—and there is no sign of joy out of the feeling of oneness. In the line "show me Division can split or pare—" the ambiguity is relational to the fear of separation and the resulting pain and inconvenience.

With the onset of the second stanza, we see, what Shaw would have said, the shades of the prison house begin to close. There is a spontaneous overflow of the moments in which the persona experiences the glory and freshness of a sudden realization. Love achieves the omnipresence of life and omnipotence of death—and simultaneously exceeds their boundaries, by virtue of its impregnable and non-destructible nature. The fear of "Division" vanishes within a moment. The persona immediately undergoes an affirmation experience of love which, against the contrast of the mood of uncertainty in the previous stanza, sounds more vital and resourceful. There is a persistent attempt to jar the mind into sudden recognition of epigrammatic lessons: Love is like Life merely longer: Love is like Death; Love is the Fellow of the Resurrection, which even in grave bears the flag of life, "Chanting 'Live'". Several other poems too have the overtones of the same affirmation consciousness:

Love is anterior to Life—
Posterior—to—Death—
Initial of Creation, and
The exponent of Earth (J. 917).

and

Love is that later Thing than Death—
More previous—than Life—
Confirms it at it's Entrance—And
Usurps it—of itself— (J. 924).

In another poem (J. 453), the poet finds love too high to climb, too deep to cross, too veiled to behold. And those who can behold Love, they "smile—and alter—and prattle—and die—." Bliss is an "Oddity without love," and God's nickname for love is Eternity.

What Emily is really doing in these poems is that she is struggling hard to make the duo-consciousness a lasting realization on the one hand, and expand it to multiple-consciousness on the other. All her love poems are a record of the stress and strain entailed during this process. Each time a natural desire to return to her intellectual-Puritan mono-consciousness blows the fuses of her soul, and the poet feels:

Before He comes We weigh the Time:
'Tis Heavy and 'tis Light.
When He depart, an emptiness
Is the prevailing Freight (J. 834).

and

Behold this little Bane—
The Boon of all alive—
As Common as it is unknown
The name of it is Love—
To lack of it is Woe—
To own of it is Wound—
Not elsewhere—if in Paradise
It's Tantamount be found— (J. 1438).

This later poem, since it is an "interim report" of a personal experience, full of paradoxes, the tone is casual and personal. The speaker is a person of wildly separated halves, who is being shuttled between duo-consciousness and mono-consciousness. The duo-consciousness gives her a startled recognition that love is a boon, huge and multi-dimensional. But mono-consciousness conceals this fact from her, and love becomes a "small bane." This is perhaps a reflection of Emily Dickinson's isolated life, which was, of course, the choice of her own temperament.

The love is common, yet unknown. Here the paradox seems to break all the rules of commonsense ; but in Dickinson's poetry, this type of tension occurs very often, when the mind possesses the weird power of being in the grip of two contradictory thoughts at the same time. As "ruthless are the gentle," and "cruel are the kind," so the want of love is "woe," and possession is "wound." Behind this common Dickinsonian technique of riddle and paradox is hidden the overwhelming emotional crisis of the persona. Her sense of reality extends as far as it becomes relative. Here all the negative elements of the consciousness—doubts, fears, and the sense of contingency—are so important that one can almost say that they are her consciousness—an expanded one.

This situation reminds us of Husserl's notion that consciousness is intentional, and not a passive mirror of things. The illumined areas are as much important as the areas of dormant passions and emotions.

But the important question still remains to be answered. How does Emily reconcile these two moods or two states of mind ? Her problem has always been Blakean : to reconcile the peak experience of "Circumference" with everyday "awareness," without belittling the authenticity of either. Anderson points out that Emily Dickinson eschewed to write philosophical poetry, "but much of her best work, exploring the various aspects of consciousness, is a subtle poetry of ideas. Since she was also a lyric poet, her aim was to achieve a fusion of thought and feeling"[2] In the light of Anderson's perceptive remark, a close look at Emily Dickinson's poems will reveal that in more than five hundred poems, she deliberately uses the emotive words like "gay", "bliss," "agony," "ache," "woe," "ecstasy", "rapture," and "transport," often paradoxically. in the same frame of poetic thought. They are neither her peak experiences, nor moments of sudden poetic realization of illumination or despair. When Blake faced the same problem, he asserted that there are two worlds : the world of day-to-day reality and the ideal or symbolic world created in myths and romances.

Coming back to Emily Dickinson, her symbolic world which may be referred to as her interior world, is invariably more real and vital than the everyday world. When she found the natural world impenetrable, and renounced society as alien to her poetic talents, she became an introvert to seek the meanings of her innermost vibrations : she sought to explore these meanings in the realm of love, reached through the routes of ecstasy :

"Go travelling with us !"
Her travels daily be
By routes of ecstasy
To Evening's Sea— (J. 1513).

In another poem (J. 1640), Emily Dickinson is determined to relinquish every other possession of life in exchange to ecstasy, and she will feel richer than any of her fellow beings, in contrast to their abject poverty caused by the lack of ecstasy.

Emily Dickinson's letters are an evidence that her home and personal friends, nature and books, including Bible, were

[2]Charles R. Anderson, *Emily Dickinson's Poetry: Stairway of Surprise.* p. 166.

sources of the greatest joy and vitality of her life. From her personal experience she knew the transfiguring capacity of Love, a term which epitomized for her the meaning of the entire existence. She wrote to Higginson : "Love is its own rescue, for we—at our supremest, are but its trembling Emblems." (L 522)

In spite of all this, it is an universally acknowledged notion of critics, without a single exception so far, that "the ecstasy of her lyrics springs from a more compulsive source...some deep personal experience of love seems behind these poems."[3]

Some thwarted love has been the central point behind a great many legends weaved and unweaved around Emily Dickinson's life. Critics have shown a great deal of interest in establishing the identity of the man Emily Dickinson supposedly loved, and loved with all her might. To go into the details of this problem as to how far these glib speculations of the critics are certifiable by the extant documentary evidence, and how far they are absurd and inconclusive, is very intriguing and equally inviting. But keeping up my promise I leave them to the biographical critics and recommend some names to the curious readers.[4]

---

[3]Anderson, p. 167.

[4]Jay Leyda's *Years and Hours with Emily Dickinson* has already been mentioned. Charles R. Anderson, David Higgins, T.H. Johnson, Pollitt Josephine, Richard B. Sewall, George F. Whicher, Richard Chase, Inder Nath Kher, Paul J. Ferlazzo, Jean McClure Mudge, Ruth Miller, and Dorothy Waugh, all these Dickinson critics have handled this problem with scholarly balance and critical acumen. The available facts and documents point to at least three deep emotional involvements Emily had at three different stages of her life. That Charles Wadsworth, Judge Otis Phillips Lord and Samuel Bowles had any definite impact on her creative life is a problem intransingent and intractable, in view of the available documentary proof (three unsent love letters in her handwriting addressed to some unidentified "Master") which is fragmentary and unhinged. It can be a dangerous sign in literary criticism to make a penetrating search of a biographical fact to find the poetic truth, especially in case of a poet like Emily Dickinson for whom the mere sense of living and the talk of life was joy enough, and life meant 'ecstasy.' When Higginson asked her in 1870 if she "felt want of employment in seclusion," she replied, "I never thought of conceiving that I could ever have the slightest approach to such a want in all future time," (L. 474) and sharpened her statement by adding that she felt

It would not be, however, correct to say that the concern with Emily Dickinson's private life is currently unfashionable. It is as much fashionable today as it has ever been. She is still portrayed as a New England nun, a curious mixture of myth and romance, and as "an heroic virgin who, in white,

she had not expressed herself strongly enough. There is a mutual evidence that she was in love with Judge Lord, but for him she never abandoned her deliberate life, though love returned remained a joy for her. She was also enamored by Samuel Bowles "Whose prance across his eye" had fascinated her.

Against all these plausible theories, Anderson's judgement is more than balanced : "It is precarious enough to use creative writings to reconstruct a love affair in the artist's life. It is even more dangerous to reverse the process and use the conjecture as a guide to the poems, for this tends to direct attention from their intrinsic value to their usefulness in filling out a supposed pattern. The reader with this interest uppermost is frequently attracted to inferior poems because he is moved by the 'autobiographical crises' he thinks he can piece out from the fragmentary sketched narrative, rather than by the poem as a work of art." (Anderson, pp. 167-68).

In addition to the above mentioned three on whom biographical critics have harped their half-cooked, brittle and episodic arguments, young Benjamin Franklin Newton's name may be understandably added, who was for sure Emily's first "preceptor" friend with whom the poets's relationship was more than casual, as around him had she once spun her youthful world. The way Benjamin affected Emily's life has generally escapedthe penetrating gaze of the "readers of her biography." The questions about life, death. and immortality, which later will become the flood subjects of her poetry, the meaning of intellectual growth, and the idea of adopting poetry as an art of redeeming her life, had first churned her mind after Benjamin had gone away irretrievably from her life. Non-conformist Emily Dickinson had for the first time asked herself—was Ben who possessed faith in God and in an unseen world, with God after death ? Months after his death had she struggled to know the state of his mind when Ben neared death, as Congregat onal Church had taught her that death "willingly" accepted was the only way to reach the Kingdom of Heaven. As a result of conscious decision, thereafter, she had started working doggedly on her verses, with the assistance of her only companion, lexicon. A tiny metaphorical tribute Emily paid to her friend years after in the concluding lines of a verse :

...the Pearl—
That slipped my simple fingers through
While just a girl at school. —(J. 299)

cloistered behind the walls of her father's house, renounced the world in order to nurture in sorrow the higher, purer love of one forever absent."[5]

A healthy consciousness is to be constantly reminded of the complex richness of its external and internal world by being fed at the streams of "newness." As we have observed earlier, in love poetry Emily Dickinson expands her duo-consciousness into multiple consciousness, and the inner-newness is produced by an interplay of the two. The poems in this process are a design, both immanent and transcendent, like Coleridges "divine analogue," and a means of creation. As the moods and forms of nature have got an almost a sacramental, or analogically metaphorical significance for Emily, similarly the imaginative experience of love is a symbolic structure for which there is no satisfactory substitute in life. The conceptual context in which love exists in her poetry fits in no discursive translation into her life-events. The relationship between her love poems and the larger contexts of her poetry (death, nature and immortality) is, in fact, so strikingly intimate that this can be called the philosophy of her poetry, or to put it more precisely in Coleridge's phrase, the figured language of (her) thought.

A close and critical examination of Emily Dickinson's representative love poems will reveal that there is a recurring pattern of imagery and metaphors in her love poems, and groups of poems are milestones in her journey from centre to circumference. Love as a poetic image assumes large dimensions of an 'Emblem,' absorbing the cycle of life, death, resurrection, and immortality. Though it may not be ostensible to a casual reader, any discerning reader of her poetry will discover that Dickinson's imagination in love poems pursues a method, a pattern, in transmitting the experience of love, which lurks below her consciousness in harmony with the logic of the imagination and the rationale of the concept.

These poems cannot be taken as a series of statements. They are, instead, a manipulation of symbols and images which owe their power to the poet's sense of belonging to

[5]Paul J. Ferlazzo *Emily Dickinson*, p. 13.

something larger than herself. This "larger than herself" composes order and unity in her seemingly paradoxical poetic personality. That is how the finest of Emily's love poems have their roots in her religious consciousness :

> Circumference thou Bride of Awe
> Possessing thou shalt be
> Possessed by every hallowed Knight
> That dares to Covet thee. (J. 1620)

This brief contextual poem is Emily's nearest approach to imaginative perception of love within the structure of her religious consciousness. The relationship of the poet's consciousness to a 'greater consciousness,' with whom the union is possible only in paradise after the mortal existence on the earth has ceased, is the major point of her conception of love. This idea gets evolved into a number of poems on the theme in a variety of ways and moods. The imagery in each poem is unexpectedly new, and maintains a freshness to the point of startling the reader's mind—"Fashion my spirit quaint—white—/ Quick—like a Liquor—Gay like light/ Meek let it be—too proud for Pride/ Baptized this Day—a Bride. (J. 473). Similarly, in the poem "A wife at Day break I shall be—" the poet says "Good Night," to "Midnight," and proceeds "unto the East, and Victory—". There, waiting for her welcome, she asks: "Sunrise—Hast thou a Flag for me ?" (J. 461).

'Circumference' is related to 'Awe' as bride to bridegroom. It can be recalled here that 'Awe' is Emily Dickinson's self ordained name for God, like Blake's Nobodaddy, or Shaw's old man in the sky, looking like the headmaster of an inferior public school. "Possessing" and "Possessed" refer to particular contexts of her creative activity. "Consciousness" 'possesses' (encompasses) the vision of the entire cosmos when it is in the state of identification with nature and universe, and gives impetus to the poet's creative imagination. But, at the same time, the possessing "Circumference' is "possesssed" (enshrouded) by a greater consciousness—God—whom the poet responds like a vestal virgin.

God courts her soul, takes it to the heaven. In the union with lover—God after death, who was abandoned and abdicated during the life time, the poet attains the vision of Biblical paradise, and its corollary, Eternity.

The image of God, the divine-lover, transporting the persona to heaven is a frequently used metaphor in Dickinson's love poetry. A simple generalization about the poetic thought of the poems belonging to this group can be that they draw on the familiar metaphor of Christ as the persona's lover. Sometimes the poet is a bride of all the three persons of the trinity—the Father, the Son, and the Holy Spirit, the "celestial Host," as the poet calls them (J. 817). In spite of being a non-conformist, Emily Dickinson could not remain uncompromisingly hostile to the concept of trinity in Christianity. Some critics had commented on Gibbon's ambivalent faith in catholicism, as if he was believing in the authenticity of a disputed document. This certainly cannot be said of Emily Dickinson. All that she could discover was that in the mixture of ideas and emotions that constitute her poetry, Christianity and Puritanism are valuable ingredients, with the notion that soul becomes immortal after death, and attains oneness with the person of God in trinity. Even in these poems Emily Dickinson's conception of immortality is centered in the lovers themselves, rather than in any theological principles :

These Fleshless Lovers met—
A Heaven in a gaze
A Heaven of Heavens—the Privilege
Of one another's Eyes— (J. 625)

* * *

Think of it Lover ! I and Thee
Permitted—face to face to be—
After a Life—a Death—we'll say—
For Death was That—
And this—is Thee— (J. 577).

* * *

Conscious am I in my chamber,
Of a shapeless friend—
He does not attest by Posture
Nor confirm—by word—

The persona's instinct esteems this "shapeless friend" as Immortality. (J. 679)

The following poem sums up this idea briefly and succinctly :

Unable are the Loved to die
For Love is Immortality,
Nay, it is Deity—
Unable they that love—to die
For Love reforms vitality
Into Divinity. (J. 809)

Thus the immortality that concerns Emily Dickinson arises directly from her connection with a second person, and never exists as an abstract or Christian condition. Emily once remarked the street that the lover travels is thenceforth divine, "incapable of turnpike aims."

In another poem, the persona, lying down in a bed made of "Awe", and placed in a ground that does not get interrupted by the "yellow noise" of the sunrise, waits for the judgement's day. (J. 829) In the same spirit, without breaking up any logical sequence, the poet can say :

To their apartment deep
To ribaldry may creep
Untumbled this abode—
By any man but God—(J. 1701)

Here "their" stands for the world of bodily impulses and sensations. At a different place, the poet calls God the "distant —stately Lover—" who woos by His son. This wooing, according to the poet, is a "Vicarious Courtship". (J. 357)

The dramatic poem "On this wondrous sea/Sailing silently," (J. 4), recognized by David T. Porter as an ordinary poem on romantic love, is actually a brief dialogue between the "thee" of the poem and the "pilot" on the subject of 'eternity'. The first stanza expresses the doubt of the persona as to which land is she being sailed. She intends to go to a shore "Where no breakers roar—/Where the Storm is over." The second stanza introduces the Pilot's voice in the poem. The persona gets reassured that she is being piloted to "the peaceful west," the land of Eternity.

Emily Dickinson's treatment of this basic concern may vary from poem to poem, but the variation is one of emphasis, and not of substance. Majority of the poems corroborate the same line of argument and excoriate the same poetic thought in multiple ways, and thereby broach new dimensions in the poet's duo-consciousness.

II

Thus, if the first fact of Emily Dickinson's love experience is the recognition of God as lover, a "dim companion" of her soul—and union with Him in Eternity, the second fact is that this union causes an emotional conversion in the poet. As the clay gets shaped and reshaped by the sculptor's hands, so the lover's "marauding hand" remoulds and erects the persona's consciousness and gives it a new form. In the peom "He touched me, so I live to know," (J. 506), structured around the same familiar myth of Christ as the lover, the persona has been touched by Christ and has "groped upon his breast." The experience is not limited to mere "touch" or groping upon. The imagery of the last three lines of the first stanza projects limitlessness of the lover in comparison to the diminutive nature of the persona, as the decidedly erotic images of "boundless," "awful sea" and "minor stream" would suggest. As the stream submerges its identity into the sea and gets its final repose, so the persona has lost its identity in the person of lover, and this experience has changed her profoundly. The second stanza would begin :

And now, I'm different from before.
As if I breathed superior air—
Or brushed a Royal Gown—
My feet, too, that had wandered so—
My Gipsy face—transfigured now—
To tenderer Renown—.

In the last two lines we see that the persona sinks down into a state of deep serenity, a kind of Buddhistic stillness—the "gipsy face" transformed into a "tender renown."

A versatile poet as Emily Dickinson is she expresses this mood with subtle nuances of tone, and feels no difficulty in finding the exact images to express her poetic sense. In one poem (J. 830) the persona returns to this world "with a tinge of that—" (world), and on the earth dwells "hesitating, half of Dust,/ And half of Day, the Bride." Bride here means the bride of Christ. In another poem the bride of Christ gets a sprightly and playful attention of the persona :

Because He loves Her
We will pry and see if she is fair
What difference is on her Face
From Features others wear. (J. 1229).

Emily Dickinson's association with this theme has got subtleties of paradox and ambiguity. She is not a thoughtless poet, to be sure: she grapples—in a few poems at least—with 'big' questions which were up for her all the time—and she struggles 'manfully' with them. Just opposite to Tennyson in "In Memoriam," whose protagonist "fought *his* doubts," and the poet could conduct *his* struggle outside the grammar and symbolism of his poetry, Emily Dickinson's struggle is very much within the framework of her poetry, enriching its ambiguous, paradoxical and conflicting nature.

The poet remains excited and serene, rises and sinks in divine ecstasy and despair, but one may have a genuine doubt if these moods are real and meaningful. They all spring from a deep-doubting consciousness, a perennial mode of Emily Dickinson's poetry. The poems "The World—stands—solemner—to me—" (J. 493); "I'm ceded—I've stopped being Theirs—"(J. 508); "I am alive—I guess—"(J. 470); and "I am ashamed—I hide—"(J. 473), are very good examples. In these poems, from a strictly logical point of view, Emily Dickinson, fettered up in her doubts, falters, stumbles and remains wedded to perturbedness. But these poems gain from the fact that there is unity in the organization of poetic thought which goes parallel to the 'mood' which is paradoxical and ambiguous.

The poem opens with a dramatic boldness :

I'm ceded—I've stopped being Theirs—
The name They dropped upon my face
With water, in the Country Church
Is finished using, now;

* * *

Baptized before without the choice,
But this time, consciously, of Grace—
Unto Supremest name— (J. 508)

We can see the bold and violent reversal of the speaker's 'first rank' which is too small before her "second Rank." She is pleased for being "Baptized" by her own conscious choice. But from the middle of the second stanza, fear, surprise, bewilderment, doubt, all products of speaker's own mind, are recapitulated, and carried till the succeeding stanza :

Called to my Full—the Crescent dropped—
Existence's whole Arc, filled up
With one small Diadem.

My Second Rank—too small the first—
Crowned—Crowing—on my Father's breast—
A half unconscious Queen—
But this time—Adequate—Erect,
With Will to choose, or to reject,
And I choose, just a Crown—

Here the intensity of the poetic mood grows out of a sense of the apparent nearness and intimate presence of what is irrevocably beyond her reach.

The poem "I am ashamed—I hide" is a dazzling imaginative experience of a bride-inebriate, charged with mental agility, idyllic beauty, and jaunty-consciousness moving amongst the babel of bright, presto images. The emotion, if there is any in the poem, is in the images. These images exist in relationship with the speaker's consciousness which has two sides, and both are real. The first is uncertain, passive and vanquished :

What right have I—to be a Bride—
So late a Dowerless Girl—
No where to hide my dazzled Face—
No one to teach me that new Grace—
Nor introduce—my Soul—

In the second phase, the persona becomes a wild congeries of bridal decorations, and steeps deep into naive illusions. All the negative emotions of the first stanza disappear, and an attitude of affirmation takes place :

Me to adorn—How—tell—
Trinket—to make Me beautiful—
Fabrics of Cashmere—
Never a Gown of Dun—more—
Raiment instead—of Pompdour—
For Me—My soul—to wear—

Fingers—to frame my Round Hair
Oval—as Feudal Ladies wore—
Far Fashions—Fair—
Skill to hold my Brow like an Earl—
Plead—like a Whippoorwill—
Prove—like a Pearl—
Then, for character—(J. 473)-

Actually, the poetic thought reaches its apogee in the clash between the persona's Christian faith and pagan longings. We can even say that the poem is concerned with providing some sort of framework for the same. Weil celebrating the ecstatic mood, she refuses to suppress reference to the Christian thoughts. For instance, during the imaginative rejoicing of the bride in big, soft, bumbling images, the concept of soul runs throughout the poem. In the first stanza, she wants to introduce her soul to the "new Grace—" i.e. God. In the second stanza, she wants "Fabrics of Cashmere" for herself as well as for her soul, "to wear." In the third stanza, the soul is introduced by another name—"character." Finally, soul, now referred to as "spirit," becomes frankly triumphant: "Fashion My Spirit quaint—white—/Meek—let it be—too proud—for Pride/ Baptized this Day—A Bride—". As a matter of fact, a great deal that is usually glossed over as decoration or atmosphere in this poem is aptly used by the poet to point up this same conflict. Emily persists on seeing the bridal-sites as religious sites, though, of course, with a pagan consciousness.

In the other two poems, (J. 470 and 493), there is a highly developed sense of self-preservation, and a strong "telepathic sixth-sense," which together bring to the persona a sudden awareness of the absolute value of life, when the immediate and intense moments of love have already brought her to the ledger of immortality—

> The World—stands—solemner—to me
> Since I was wed—to Him—
> A modesty befits the soul
> That bears another's—name—

And immediately afterwards, we feel as if there is a "bisection" of the self. In these numb and quiet moments, shə becomes aware of her individuality, strength and durability:

> A doubt—if it be fair—indeed—
> To wear that perfect—pearl—
> The Man—upon the Women—binds—
> To clasp her soul—for all—

By the end, the doubtful tone becomes totally ambiguous :

> A Gratitude—that such be true—
> It had esteemed the Dream—
> Too beautiful—for Shape to prove—
> Or posture—to redeem ! (J. 493).

In "I am alive—I guess—," though the persona has already "stepped in Immortality," the subjective element is more emphatic and powerful than her religious identification. The poem is replete with images which guarantee her a life, filled with moments of great excitement, because feeling peaceful means not feeling really alive :

I am alive—I guess—
The Branches on my Hand
Are full of Morning Glory—
And at my finger's end—

The Carmine—tingles warm—
And if I hold a Glass
Across my Mouth—it blurs it—
Physician's—proof of Breath—

Further, the persona is living in a "Parlor," and not in a "Room," "So Visitors may come—/ And lean—and view it sidewise—." This arrangement—perhaps—because she does not want to break her contact with the world from which she has stepped out. Moreover, she is not in possession of "a House," in order that her life may not get delimited only to herself. Though the speaker is feeling immensely happy for being alive, and not only alive, but "Alive—twofold The Birth I had—/ And this—besides, in—Thee!", she prefers not to drop her maiden name :

And marked my Girlhood's name—
So Visitors may know',
Which Door is mine—and not mistake—
And try another Key—(J. 470).

Here, Emily Dickinson's ability to bring into focus several diverse sense-impressions to prove the continuity of life, in spite of becoming one with God and attaining immortality, lends additional dimensions and depth to the poem. A series of firm and concrete images bring out a valid, rounded, and fully realized appreciation of life. The persona's strong craving for touch reminds the reader of Keats who said "touch has a memory." In "I felt my iife with both my hands (J. 351), the tactile quality gives a three-dimensional grasp to the imagery. On the whole, this poem is a fine example of a centering in Dickinson's imagery of the various qualities of an object (here the various impressions of Life in a post-mortal stage, i. e., immortality), into a single apperception. In this particular poem, life emerges as a totality, with all its glory, warmth and, freshness.

A large number of Emily Dickinson's love poems carry lively pictures of nature objects : sea, moon, daisy, sun, brook, ocean, peninsula, the "invisible-mainland", rose, harebell, bees, bobolinks, and many other small but significant units of nature. All these are, like the bride and bridegroom images, Emily Dickinson's poetic parallels of the relationship between her mono-consciousness, and duo-consciousness, and the ultimate expansion of the two into facile but transitory multiple-consciousness :

Because the Bee May blameless hum
For Thee a Bee do I become
List even upto Me.

Because the Flowers unafraid
May lift a look on thine, a Maid
Always a Flower would be

Nor Robins, Robins, need not hide
When Thou upon their Crypts intrude
So wings bestow on Me
Or Petals, or a Dower of Buzz
That Bee to ride, or Flower of Furze
I that way worship Thee. (J. 869).

The influence of male upon the female—a mixture of physical attraction, fascination, infatuation, and awe—are emphasized here analogically. In another poem (J. 1339) the rose is left with an ecstatic rapture (interfused with humility) of intense love-experience, after Bee, the lover, finishes his courtship and "their Moment (is) consummated."

Remained for him—to flee—
Remained for her—of rapture
But the humility. (J. 1339)

In these poems, she aims to paint nature to produce the sense of oneness between her consciousness and the objects of nature. It is an attempt to bypass the level of separation of human personality from the nature objects. Here we can follow very closely the phenomenology of Emily Dickinson's poetic experience *en route* to heaven.

III

Dickinson's characteristic tendency in all of these groups is to embody her secular themes of physical love in religious images, and to embody her religious themes of spiritual love in images of the flesh and the physical world. Thus, she creates the tension that is found in the best of her love poems : a tension between the claims of the physical love of a mortal and the divine love of God, between the "Sumptuous Moment" of this world and the timelessness of the next, between experience and abstract idea. Emily Dickinson's love peoms dramatize these opposing forces with poetic sensitivity and considerable technical skill.

William Dean Howells in a review of Emily Dickinson's poems in 1891 wrote: "There is no hint of what turned her life upon itself, and probably this was its natural evolution or involution, from tendencies inherent in the New England, or the Puritan, spirit."[6] Mabel Loomis Todd made more or less the same observation a few years later : "She had tried society and the world, and found them lacking.... Her life was the normal blossoming of a nature introspective to a high degree, whose best thought could not exist in pretence."[7] Bt a time when Emily wrote her intensest love poems, she, like Thoreau, had already decided to live with the bare essentials of life. Thoreau had gone to Waldon Pond. Emily sought the universe within herself, and poetry writing became for her an art, a dedication. To Mrs. Holland, she wrote in 1877: "Had we the first intimation of the Definition of Life, the Calmest of us would be Lunatics !" (L.II, 576). Like

---

[6]William Dean Howells, "The Editor's Study," *Harper's Magazine*, LXXXII (January 1891), 318. Quoted in Bingham, *Ancestors Brocades*, p. 96.

[7]*Poems* by *Emily Dickinson*, Second Series, edited by two of her friends, T.W. Higginson and Mabel Loomis Todd (Boston, 1891), Preface. Reprinted in Bingham, *Ancestors' Brocades*, pp. 417-19.

Thoreau, Emily too felt triumphant in her individuality, and, by contrast, "quiet desperation" of ordinary lives.

It is the supreme triumph of individuality which becomes royalty in Emily Dickinson's love poetry. She always remains uncrowned, without a final union, "the Queen Recluse," as Samuel Bowles called her. Renunciation of the visible world makes her inner perceptions more subjective in their appeal. Emily defends herself in verse : "My best Acquaintances are those/with whom I spoke no Word—" (J. 932).

It is due to this total commitment to individuality that her love poems often become meditative and mystic in their theme and content. Each of these poems can attain its full terms of appreciation only if it can be viewed as a personal spiritual exercise—the byproduct of a process rather than an illumination of a lived and consumed moment :

—the belief that Somewhere—
Within the Clutch of Thought—
There dwells one other Creature
Of Heavenly Love—forgot— (J. 532).

The experience of love, residing within the clutch of thought, becomes for her a single moment of illumination in which her senses, intellect and the emotions, all integrated, create the meditative mood. That is why most of her love poems have a close-up effect, as if reality was being seen through a microscope :

At Half past Seven, Element
Nor Implement, be seen—
And *Place* was where the *Presence* was
Circumference between. (J. 1084)

Love usually ends in union, but her life had taught her just the opposite, and she had got into the habit of thinking separation as something permanent. Then she keeps on struggling to catch the affirmation-experience, in each phase recreated and refabricated. Again and again the poet's self is dramatized either against fictive settings or against vividly real situations.

It is against a special perspective of these conditions that Emily Dickinson's love poetry becomes highly personal, and the individual poems, instead of becoming a means of public communication, end as an exercise in private discipline and personal glory. In these poems the development of sensibility is such that it comprehends and apprehends her whole unseen world of mind and soul. These are Dickinson's implicit poetics which guide us in an understanding of her poetry.

CHAPTER IV

Religious Experience

I

The poetry of Emily Dickinson is an attempt, every time renewed, to give an answer to the perennial question of the problem of here and hereafter. The problem became more intense because of a conflict between the critical rationalism and the urge for mystic ıealization. She ever remained suspect of the idea of bodily resurrection. The Biblical doctrine of post-mortal immortality did not sound to her as true, though she always felt concerned with the idea of mmortality as a means of victory against the transient nature of life and time. Her religion had obviously given her a sacramental interpretation of death and immortality, of universe and God. And therefore her concern with immortality was a natural sequence of her bewilderment with death.

Immortality as understood by Emily Dickinson was not a dogma It was a metaphysical truth based on her direct experience of death. Her religious heritage indicated it but did not prove anything conclusively. Dickinson's concept of immortality has an intimate association with her concepts, of God and religion. The central issues are again revolving around the problem of a coordination of conflicting experiences into a single unified vision.

A deeply religious poet as Emily Dickinson is, immorality remained her concern to the verge of obsession, a "flood subject" as she herself called it. When she picked up Biblical myths to form the structure of her poems, she frequently turned to the passages in Corinthians and Revelation.[1] Paul's remark that "we now see in a riddle"

[1]Passages from Corinthians and Revelation are usually read at funeral services.

has got frequent echoes in her poetry with recurrent images of "Riddle" and "Disc."

Yet another glance at her poetry will confirm that the doctrine of eternal happiness in heaven after death did not impress Dickinson. But this resistance did not give her any feeling of relief or superiority. In many of her poems she wishfully regrets for her non-conformist attitude. For Emily Dickinson with an abandoned belief in Church, God and the Bible, poetry became an essence for the redemption of life. Neither with any desire for Pater's religion of art, nor in agreement with Santayana's insistence on a greatly enlarged role for poetry and imagination in place of formal religion ; Emily Dickinson experienced the crisis of old religion dying and a new one imminent. Her mind naturally reverted to myth[2]. Poetry became for her a means of establishing the relation of her soul to what she conceived as Absolute Reality—a theme which occupied her from first to last. Behind the playful and sporting attitude towards this Absolute Reality (God) in her poetry, there is a clear-out manifestation of sincere and abiding faith :

At least—to pray—is left—is left—
Oh Jesus—in the Air—
I know not which thy chamber is—
I am knocking everywhere— (J. 502)

While thinking of God, she very often wears the mask of a child. Her mood is generally surcharged with humour, wit, irony, and paradox, along with a mixture of sophistication and innocence :

"Heavenly Father"—take to thee
The Supreme iniquity

[2]The word "myth" is used here not to mean the fairy tales or things that are not true. The word is used here in its original sense in which Plato used it. Plato means by myth a form of expression to which one turns when the resource of the intellect have been exhausted, and one still has something of immense importance and significance which one must express somehow.

Fashioned by thy candid Hand
In a moment contraband—
Though to trust us—seem to us
More respectful—"We are Dust"—
We apologize to thee
For thine own duplicity— (J. 1461).

Because Emily Dickinson's idea about God is that of "A supreme power," the moments of her intimate relationship with God are those in which "death" (loss of the vision of "Circumference") brings about the poignant realization of God's existence :

The first Day's Night had come—
And grateful that a thing
So terrible—had been endured—
I told my soul to sing—

She said her Strings were snapt—
Her Bow—to Atoms blown—
And so to mend her—gave me work
Until another Morn— (J. 410)

Here "Day" stands for a vision of "Circumference" and "night" for the loss of that vision. Though the poet feels happy that she could survive that loss, the signs of loss are lingering yet : "Strings snaps and Bow blown," and a mending therefore is required. In one of her poems (J. 947) the persona asks the cause of the tolling bells and gets the reply in a "lonesome tone" that "a soul had gone to God." Persona then comments that the bells should not have been "tolled" but "rung" because the departure of a soul to heaven is a happy event, and this "good news" should be given in a "proper way."

Jacob's story in the Bible who wrestled with an angel throughout the night and defeated it, and in the morning discovered that it was God, fascinated Emily Dickinson so much that she frequently refers to this story in her poems and letters. We will examine two of her poems on this theme in detail.

A little East of Jordan,
Evangelists record,
A Gymnast and an Angel
Did wrestle long and hard—

Till morning touching mountain—
And Jacob, waxing strong
The Angel begged permission
To Breakfast—to return—

Not so, said cunning Jacob !
"I will not let thee go
Except thou bless me"—Stranger !
The which acceded to—

Light swung the silver fleeces
"Peniel !" Hills beyond,
And the bewildered Gymnast
Found he had worsted God ! (J. 59).

Two Swimmers wrestled on the spar—
Until the morning sun—
When One—turned smiling to the land—
Oh God ! the Other One !

The stray ships—passing—
Spied a face—
Upon the waters borne—
With eyes in death—still begging raised—
And hands—beseeching—thrown! (J. 201).

These poems recreate the story of the Biblical wrestler Jacob[3] who wrestles with an angel during the night, and

[3]Genesis 32, verses 24-30, in the Bible refer to the story of Jacob, wrestling with a man during the night. The man feels weak against Jacob, and in the morning, defeated, begs Jacob's permission to let him go. But by this time Jacob has discovered that the man is no one other than God. So he says, "I will not let thee go, except thou bless me." God blesses Jacob and disappears. "And Jacob called the name of the place Pe-ni-ce: for I have seen God face to face, and my life is preserved."

wins over. He is not aware who the other wrestler is. In the morning it is realized that the other wrestler is God Himself. And with this realization the poetic thought of the two poems parts company. The poems quoted were written in 1859 and 1850 and published in 1914 and 1890, respectively (Johnson). The second poem being more precise in its thought and imagery, naturally got the publishers' attention first.

The poetic experience of the first poem, as we see, is very simple and free of tension. The content of the poem is almost an exact representation of the Biblical story. There is not much "poetic" improvement on the idea behind it, except that Jacob is given adjectives "cunning" and "bewildered." Jacob may be "cunning" because he adeptly makes full use of the opportunity by asking God to bless him; and "bewildered" perhaps at God's merciful attitude towards him. From the point of view of poetic technique the last stanza is very remarkable. It employs the same technique as we have seen in "A route of Evanescence." Instead of stating the idea directly, that God blessed Jacob and disappeared behind the hill, the esssence of the idea is conveyed in two brief and refreshingly new images—"Light Swung the silver fleeces." Both "Light" and "Silver fleeces" are the images of brightness and they amply depict the joyful mental state of the blessed one, Jacob. Thus, rather than striving after the logic of the poetic thought, the reader is expected to see the images of the speeding light and the silver fleece to get the essence of it.

Coming back to the second poem, the reader is simply left amazed by the intensity and condensation. The same story, same theme, Emily is able to recreate with what intensity and condensation! The profundity and precision of the last four lines of the poem can "freeze" any sensitive reader, as Emily Dickinson would like them to.

The first stanza yields to a literal reading. The same story is narrated in less space (two lines) as compared to the previous poem. This time a new image, which is of the sea, is introduced in the background. The wrestlers (Jacob and the angel) are introduced as swimmers. Then the same course—fighting—until the morning. From the third line, the Biblical myth becomes the poetic myth of Dickinson. It is reconstructed to give an appropriate structure to the thought Emily wants to convey. She, the non-conformist, is concerned with her own fate. Like Jacob wrestling with God, Emily has been struggling with her own religious faith. This time God does not bless Jacob. She will pray, but her prayer may be turned down.[4] In the original story, God is defeated. But here, it is the other way round—"When one turned smiling to the land—/Oh God! the Other One:" And then, even the narrator is left stultified. Once again, the logic of metaphor rather than the logic of syllogism will be employed. In the line "Oh God ! the Other One", the narrator's sense of wonder, interfused with an inner terror and a mood of uncertainty, can be sensed.

The stanza introduces a number of images, all ambiguous, yet picturesque, and not having any direct discursive relationship to the reference point given in the first stanza. The emotive relation is, of course, there. The only image that is common in both the stanzas is that of water, which forms the background of the poem. The "stray ships—passing—" conveys the idea of the continuity of normal life which goes on in its normal course in spite of the all-pervading hand of "death" present there.

The images of "sea" (the presence of "ships" and "spar" in the first line warrants that the sea is in the background) and "ships" moving quite indifferently make the poetic thought very penetrating and moving. The movement of the ships is proud and magnificent, which goes well with the vastness of the sea. On the contrary the dead one is presented through inert and precise images in the form of pictures. First of all, only the "face," with no other description of it. Next come the "eyes" asking for forgiveness. One can grasp the emotion of regret and the need for redemption so much deep drown into the narrator's consciousness that even death

[4]Of Course—I prayed—
And did God care ?
He cared as much as on the Air
A Bird—had stamped her foot— (J. 376).

has not been able to decompose them. Lastly, the image of the "hands" requesting for a pardon again.

All these images are full-fledged pictures, each depicting the same emotion. Markedly, there is no voice in this stanza —no sound at all. The whole scene is made out of the pictures flat, unmoving and quiet, to be recognized only through the emotions depicted and not by the outlines of color. Moreover, instead of getting the whole view, the reader just gets the essence of the consciousness of the dead one the emotions felt at the time of death—horror, and an eventual feeling of surrender with eyes "begging" and hands "beseeching." The "stray ships—walking" lend a sense of ease, emotional isolation, or nonchalance. But as the reader moves along with the verse, the atmosphere seems to be surcharged with tension. Each phase of the consciousness of the person lying down in death is presented through picturesque images which emphasizes the emotional effect more and more solemnly. The last word "thrown" leaves the reader with a feeling of anguish and emptiness. The prayer is turned down, and the dead one is not redeemed.

On its literal level, the poem creates an experience of the final destiny of the person who wrestles with God. Emily Dickinson has used this Biblical myth to project her own emotions—a fear of her own destiny as a nonbeliever. Another point about the structure of the imagery is that the poet purposely gives juxtaposed images in the same stanza, perhaps to enhance the sensory impression and the subtlety of the emotion. The first few images are those of size and structure—"Stray—ship," a concrete and direct image with very little emotive appeal. In sharp contrast to the above comes the dead person lying on the surface of the water, whose body is pictured in degrees. Our attention is invited only to one part at a time. This technique enhances the emotional appeal of the poem.

It, however, remains to be decided as to why a theme which creates such emotional crisis became a stubborn theme with Emily Dickinson.[5] Perhaps it gives vent to the

[5]In one of the very latest letters that Emily Dickinson wrote to

religious crisis Emily herself was facing in her matured years.

II

At some places in her poetry, she compares Bible "unfavourably" with Orpheus, whose music only "Captivates" and does not "Condemn."

Sin—a distinguished Precipice
Others must resist—
Boys that "believe" are very lonesome—
Other Boys are "lost"—
Had but the Tale a warbling Teller
All the Boys would come—
Orpheus' Sermon captivated—
It did not condemn— (J. 1545).

At another occasion she refers to Cupid, the God of love, as an "authentic deity," and concludes that God and love are synonymous; how can God be love's "adversary!"

By all this and more that we see in her poetry, Emily Dickinson means that religion is not just a ritual or a sacrament which she can accept or reject in predictable terms. Religion for her means an experience of the consciousness which she should be able to feel with the whole of her body and heart, mind and soul And if her doctrinal Christianity fails to give her that experience (ecstasy, transport, Paradise—her frequent terms for it), she is capable of creating her own type of religious experience, as authentic and involving as the religion of her family, which she too was taught.

This new type of religious experience is a state of "heightened consciousness," related in her imagination with the terms "centre" and the "circumference." During her experience of this religion of consciousness, Emily Dickinson attains a complete identificaton with nature, and comes to

---

Higginson, presumably in early spring 1886, shortly before her death, she comments on her increasing illness, concluding with a note of affectionate remembrance for Higginson and his family thus :

"Audacity of Bliss," said Jacob to the Angel, "I will not let thee go except I bless thee" —Pugilist and Poet, Jacob was correct—" T.H. Johnson in *Poems of Emily Dickinson,* Vol. I, p. 45.

terms with the world from which she keeps herself shut otherwise. Nature, which the circumference of her consciousness can surround now, becomes, for her, the Paradise. In this Paradise of her imagination, completely entwined with her psyche, every natural object is given a human shape and human meaning. It is not indifferent like the paradise of the Bible. This vision of her own "paradise" leads her to a mythical experience and makes her imagination mythopoeic. Her mythopoeic imagination is quite capable of conceiving within it a vision of the universe whose laws are different from the laws of the universe we are living in. The inhabitants of this universe are able to make their moments of bliss eternal :

There is a morn by men unseen--
Whose maids upon remoter green
Keep their Seraphic May—
And all day long, with dance and game,
And gambol I may never name—
Employ their holiday.

Here to light measure, move the feet
Which walk no more the village street—
Nor by the wood are found –
Here are the birds that sought the Sun
When last year's distaff idle hung
And summer's brows were bound.

Ne'er saw I such a wondrous scene—
Ne'er such a ring on such a green—
Nor so serene array—
As if the stars some summer night
Should swing their cups of Chrysolite—
And revel till the day—

Like thee to dance—like thee to sing—
People upon that mystic green--
I ask, each new May Morn.
I wait thy far, fantastic bells—
Announcing me in other dells—
Unto the different dawn ! (J. 24).

In this poem the world we live in and the world of the people of "mystic green" stand over against each other. The laws of nature in both the worlds are not the same. What the "mystic green" and the "remote green" would mean to the speaker is conveyed through the imagery of the poem. It is a world of richness and vitality—"with dance and game,/And gambol".../Employ their holiday;" of deep sensousness, of natural beauty and fertility—"As if the stars some summer night/Should swing their Chrysolite—/And revel till the day—." It appeals to the imagination, and has its own freshness, identity, and lasting vitality—"Whose maids upon remoter green/Keep their Seraphic May—."

In an ordinary state of consciousness, we see the world as objective, as something set over against us. When she says, "Bible deals with Centre and her business is circumference," she implies that Bible deals with man in his isolated state from God which only God can cross. It is in the state of isolation when man's consciousness is something different from the objective world, the world is not a part of him. The world which Bible prescribes for her is the one which promises an Eden after death, an Eden in which man will live eternally. There are assumptions of salvation and damnation, but all these aspects of Bible have got a big question mark for Emily. They are not related to her consciousness in anyway. Nothing responds to her. Its morals and intelligence she cannot grasp because it does not have a human shape and human meaning for her.

For Emily, religion must be something which she will be able to accept in a mood of complete peacefulness and joy. Such moods of complete identification, when she will feel that God is a part of her and she a part of God, she can't achieve in the ordinary state of consciousness when the split between her emotions and the intellect is not completely off and she feels alien and foreign to everything. This feeling of separation, her encounter with the "Centre," as she calls it, makes her feel that "this is not a part of me." And it soon becomes this is not the way she wants. Consequently, she turns to myth to create a cosmology of her own and to have an experience of "circmference." Under this new religious consciousness she will meet her God on her own uncompromising terms. For her, the difference between the religion she has, and the religion she wants to have, is very tense. She cannot surrender herself to an objective religion. She wants to be at home with her own religion.

"Home is the definition of God" she said once, and "home" is inside the "circumference" of one's own being. In this state the mind feels immortal The word "home" has become an archetypal symbol in Emily Dickinson's religious poetry. She uses it variantly for Immortality, God, and Heaven. Her poems "The feet of People Walking Home" (J. 7), "Tho' I get Home—how late—How late—" (J. 207), "I Years Had been from Home" (J. 609), all the three use the same archetypal image, *i.e.*, "home", in different situations. The context, however, remains the same—poet's need for home, *i.e.*, need for God.

In "The Feet of People Walking Home," Dickinson shows a traditional undoubting approach to Christianity and to the immortality that it offers. "Home" in this poem stands for "heaven" as the use of "sandals" in line 2 (with Biblical connotations) and "Crocus" in line 3 will indicate. "Crocus" is an early spring flower, symbolizing resurrection. "Crocus" rises after remaining in the bondage of snow. Winter clearly represents "Death." The third stanza reinforces the antithesis of reason and faith :

My figures fail to tell me
How far the village lies—
Whose peasants are the Angels—
Whose cantons dot the skies— (J. 7).

The distance of the heaven cannot be calculated, as we can calculate the distances of the earth. The image of the heaven is expanded here in a wide space, "the village." We see it with all its glory and magnificence, "Angels," and the sky broken up into states—"cantons dot the skies." At the end of the poem it is concluded that the poet succumbs to an unquestionable adoration of the "unknowable—'that Dark' "—and to the Christian concepts of resurrection and immortality in the heaven. In this poem, the speaker's thoughts are more important than the physical presence.

The other poem "Tho' I get home how late—how late—" (J. 207) is more elusive in its tone, and more dramatic in the way it conveys the poetic thought.

The locale is the consciousness of the poet. The persona is imagining how "transporting that moment" will be—a moment which is "brewed from decades of Agony," when she will reach "home." It will be quite late, but the fact that she is reaching, though late, will more than compensate for her belated arrival. She imagines that it will be night "descending,—dumb—and dark," and the inhabitants of the house, angels perhaps, will be found waiting for her, and it will be a moment of "Extasy".

In the second stanza, the persona comes still closer to the "idea" of home. The "knock" is over : she has entered the "home" and joined people there. In this stanza, we see the inside of the house. The persona feels that she will perhaps regret for her delay in returning home : "To think just how the fire will burn." This fire is the fire of remorse, a sense of guilt and subsequent regret. She also does not know what look she will find in the eyes of "God" whom she had been deceiving for a long time by her disbelief and religious antagonism. She does not even know what excuses she will give for her delay, and what response she is likely to get. While thinking "how long—cheated eyes will turn—" "What myself will say," and what "itself will say to me—," the persona is totally lost in the thought of these doubts and questionings, and passes endless time on the way—"Beguiles the centuries of way !"

The poet is on her way "home," and the poem is an imaginative re-creation of the situation, characters, and attitudes, she is likely to face there. What is remarkable here is that the poet is moving ahead for an endless journey which may take her centuries even. The destination is not yet reached. It is not even in sight.

Finally, the poet reaches "home." "I years had been from Home" (J. 609) starts with the speaker of the poem standing at the door, replete with a host of fears, doubts and speculations, not having the courage to knock and enter. The first poem had a big heaven "the village" with its angels : the second, a "home" with a few residents : "they...expecting me." In the poem under discussion, it is just one "door" and one "Face," "a Face I never saw before."

> I years had been from Home
> And now before the Door
> I dared not enter, lest a Face
> I never saw before
>
> Stare stolid into mine
> And ask my Business there—
> "My Business but a Life I left
> Was such remaining there?"
>
> I leaned upon the Awe—
> I lingered with before -
> The second like an Ocean rolled
> And broke against my ear—
>
> I laughed a crumbling Laugh
> That I could fear a Door
> Who Consternation compassed—
> And never winced before—
>
> I fitted to the Latch
> My Hand, with trembling care
> Lest back the awful Door should Spring
> And leave me in the Floor—
>
> Then moved my Fingers off
> As cautiously as Glass
> And held my ears, and like a thief
> Fled gasping from the House— (J. 609).

A simple paraphraseable content of the first two stanzas is that the speaker had been away from "Home" for a number of years. When she has finally reached at the door, she is scared to enter as she may not get a welcome, and be questioned "why she came". To this question, the speaker has already thought of a ready reply that she came to collect "the Life" she had left many years ago, provided it was still there, and was not lost. In these stanzas, the experience of the narrator, a fictitious fear, is presented logically, diramacally, and in a quizzical manner.

The language here has conventional signs and context to convey the meaning, which can be grasped more effectively by a close study of her other poems on the same theme. The narrator successfully builds up fictive emotions which will have a bearing on the poem's theme and imagery to the last.

After the dialogue between the speaker and the "Face" (she expects to meet at "Home") is over, the poem becomes quite ambiguous in its tone and imagery. There seems to be a sure shift in the emotional condition of the narrator, who is depicted as quick-witted, confident, self-conscious, and self-assured. The wit of the narrator in the second stanza, "My Business but a Life I left/was such remaining there !" stands in sharp contrast to the emotions expressed in the third stanza. The situation by now has already become highly dramatic and gone beyond the narrator's control. In the lines "I leaned upon the Awe/I lingered with Before," the emotions of the narrator are dramatized, and the physical identity becomes quite unimportant. Fear, the illusional reality of the opening few lines, becomes the dominant emotion of the present situation.

Awe, Emily Dickinson's term for God of the "religion of her consciousness," is ever present to rescue her, in case her own God rejects her. Awe, with whom she only used to "linger," is vehemently needed by her in these moments of deep emotional crisis, at a closer level, and she now "leans" against Him. In the next two lines, once again, there is a quick and sudden change in the poetic thought. We are directed to witness a totally new situation, which is elusive, emotive, and highly fictitious. This situation is fitted into a sequence of abstract images and complex symbols. In the lines, "The Second line an ocean rolled/And broke against my ear—" the technique of paradox is employed to convey the intended poetic meaning of the speaker. The speaker perhaps means to communicate an abiding, deep and encompassing impact of a second's mystical realization.

In her original version of the poem written in 1862, (the text adopted here 1872) Emily had given "Silence" for "Second." If we adopt the original text, the paradox becomes more apparent: the "Silence" breaking against the sense of sound, *i.e.*, "Ear." If we adopt the second reading her "Second" perhaps will mean a unit of Time. Paradox still remains intact. "Second" is a very small unit of time. Nevertheless, it is so much volcanic in its appeal, in the present context, that it is felt like an ocean rolling.

The line "And broke against my ear" may make one feel that the persona undergoes some mystical experience for the split of a second, and then comes out of it loaded with courage and confidence to face Home, God, and other tensions of the situation. The next stanza certifies this point.

The mood of the poem, the setting, and the narrative, once again, become superbly dramatic. The tension of the preceding lines suddenly breaks down, and the persona, who was "lingering" and "leaning" against "Awe" asserts its roaring strength. The paraphrase of these lines will read like this: "I laughed at my fear and weakness. I, who can encompass terror, confusion, and dismay (into the boundaries of my consciousness), who has never been affected or moved by pain, who has never felt restive, how can be afraid of a simple door !"

The regained vitality and strength bring her to the point of touching the latch of the door to open it. But with a sudden and quick change of emotion, the narrator's consciousness plunges once again into the dark realms of fear and dismay. She tries to open it with great care and fear, lest it should fall back on her and destroy her. Though the fear felt and unfelt a number of times was fictitious (the drama of fear and courage following each other cyclically takes place in narrator's consciousness only), it has really worked out. Her courage is defeated and the persona flies away in the end.

From the second stanza onwards, the speaker's consciousness passed through a number of dramatic situations, or is itself dramatized, to be more precise. The climax of the poetic thought is in its tone, full of consternation, emotive conflict, irony, and paradox. Tone also adds meaning to the experience created, which is neither regretful, nor resigned, but highly stoical. At every step of the poem we see the creation of an illusional reality. Symbols like "Awe,"

"Home," "Life," and "crumbling laugh" are surrogates for the concepts and objects to which they refer.

Though the poem presents a religious theme, we do not see the speaker in a mood of regret, prayer, or apology. On the other hand, the statement that she has come to take the "life," intensifies the awareness that she has not come for a surrender. The poem, on the whole, presents the fluid image of a person terrorised, still not engaged in any fervent prayer. Till the end, she is not chastened to the humility of the "half-plea" and "half-hope." It is a situation of "no plea and no hope."

Though the contextual references of this poem are a little bit complex, it is through them that the poem attains its ironical meaning. Even in a mood of despair and terrorised by the dictates of the scriptural notations, Emily does not demand that God, the owner of the house here, should give her grace and confidence that she needs for her salvation. The language and the metaphors used reveal the poet's thoughts, feelings, and exhibit her state of spiritual crisis. As she goes ahead with her speculations (in the poem), her consciousness moves reversely, and finally it budges off from the door of God.

III

Emily Dickinson's religion of a heightened consciousness is based, not on the arguments, but on suggestive images which she calls "the emblem." The metaphors, symbols, images, that she employs to convey that experience are emblems in her poetry, as we have seen in the discussion just concluded. She calls human beings "the trembling emblems of love." Another very important aspect of her experience with "circumference" is that the circumference of human consciousness is surrounded by a still greater consciousness. Poet's own relationship with this consciousness is like that of the bride to the bridegroom, sea to the moon, daisy to the sun, etc. All these are recurring images in her poetry :

The Drop that wrestles in the Sea—
Forgets her own locality—
As I—toward Thee— (J. 284)

and

Exultation is the going
Of an inland soul to sea,
Past the houses—past the headlands—
Into deep Eternity. (J. 76).

Sometimes poet's own soul is a "peninsula" which is attached to an "invisible mainland." Emily Dickinson gives the name "Awe" to this greater consciousness. Thus "Awe" is her common name for God. "Awe" is the divine lover to whom the feminine poet responds :

Circumference thou Bride of Awe
Possessing thou shalt be
Possessed by every hallowed Knight
That dares to covet thee— (J. 1620).

and

To their apartment deep
No ribaldry may creep
Untumbled this abode
By any man but God, (J. 1701).

"Awe" is not the dogmatic Christian God. Consequently, paganism in her is not affected by "Awe". Emily Dickinson comes very close to English romantic poets in her belief that "Awe" is not a stern jealous God : and He will not mind if there are separate "gods" for each mold of nature :

If "All is possible with him"
As he besides concedes
He will refund us finally
Our confiscated Gods— (J. 1260).

"Awe" can even be a female : "I always ran Home to Awe when a child... He was an awful Mother, but I liked him better than none," Emily Dickinson once remarked.

As a Christian, Emily Dickinson identifies "Awe" with the third person of the Trinity, the Holy Spirit. Biblical symbols for the holy spirit are the "bird" and the "wind". And these two are very common images in Emily Dickinson's poetry. She recognizes "Awe" by its movement in her soul, like a "tide" moving in the "sea". Her God is not a recluse like a Puritan God, who cannot be seen by anybody. He is the innermost secret of her consciousness.

The Bible says that man will regain Paradise after death and will live in it eternally thereafter. For Emily Dickinson, the boundaries of her Paradise are within her own mind ; the charms of heaven in the bush are superseded by charms of heaven in the hand. Her paradise is given to her by her experience of the circumference :

Going to Heaven !
I don't know when—
Pray do not ask me how !
Indeed I am too astonished
To think of answering you !
Going to Heaven !
How dim it sounds !
And yet it will be done
As sure as flocks go at the night
Unto the shepherd's arm ! (J. 79)

and

I've known a Heaven, like a Tent—
To wrap it's shinning Yards—
Pluck up it's stakes, and disappear—
Without the Sound of Boards. (J. 243)

In this type of religious experience the poet sometimes visits some mystical unknown lands. An essential quality of a mystic poet is perhaps a realization of the vision of eternity —and its acceptance as truth. To a mystic eternity does not mean an endless time ; it means "a present," "a now," which absorbs all possible hereafters. In quite a few poems the persona visits a mystical unknown land, and comes back with a few flashes of the other world in the memory :

Just lost, when I was Saved !
Just felt the world go by !
Just girt me for the onset with Eternity,
When breath blew back,

And on the other side
I heard recede the disappointed tide !

Therefore, as One returned, I feel,
Odd secrets of the line to tell !
Some Sailor, skirting foreign shores—
Some pale Reporter, from the awful doors
Before the Seal !

Next time, to stay !
Next time, the things to see
By Ear unheard,
Unscrutinized by Eye—

Next time, to tarry,
While the Ages steal—
Slow tramp the Centuries,
And the Cycles wheel ! (J. 160)

In Emily Dickinson's poetry "summer" and "noon" are the symbols of an eternal state of consciousness :

There's a certain slant of light,—
Winter Afternoons—
That oppresses ; like the Heft
Of Cathedral Tunes—

* * *

When it comes, the Landscape listens—
Shadows—hold their breath—
When it goes, 't is like the Distance
On the look of Death— (J. 258)

In spite of all this, Emily Dickinson could not be a complete mystic. One simple reason can be the rationalism of her age which must have affected her directly or indirectly. The second, and more powerful, is the Puritan background, with its insistence that Divine 'Will' is a law unto itself, and that it makes sense only to a believer. No human mind can experience or penetrate it. It can be held by faith and not by experience.

This exactly is the central point of conflict in Emily's complex poetic consciousness—a conflict between her poetic longings and her faith. She experiences it very poignantly when she says : "Consciounesss is the only home of which we now know."

Next comes the paradox of Emily Dickinson's poetic imagination. Her experience of "Awe" and communion with nature gives her a sense of "division" or "bisection" within. A part of her mind is mortal, and a part is immortal. Both must, however, go through death to achieve eternity. In one poem ("Conscious am I in my Chamber," J. 679), she speaks of the indwelling spirit as the immortal part of herself. In these moments of bisection, sometimes, the distinction is between the poet herself and her soul ; sometimes between her soul and her mind, and other times between her soul and her consciousness. In one poem the soul is attended by a single hound which is its own identity. She does not accept the Platonic view that the soul is immortal by its very nature.

Thus the first major fact of her religious experience is the vision of the earth as heaven, as we have been explaining and illustrating so far. The second fact, which is equally important, is that the vision is not permanent. It is transient, evanescent,—it comes and goes. When it comes, it is a sunny and a golden time for the poet, a heaven on earth,—and eternal summer, a noon, a state which she expresses in so many ways. This vision is an experience ; it comes and goes unpredictably. That is why she often symbolizes this vision through the metaphors of drunkenness :

Inebriate of Air am I
And Debauchee of Dew
Reeling thro endless summer days—
From inns of Molten Blue— (J. 214)

and

Bred as we, among the mountains,
Can the sailor understand
The divine intoxication
Of the first league out from land? (J. 76).

Whatever may be the traditional symbols for liquor leading

this state of drunkenness, Emily Dickinson symbolizes it by "Domingo," "ManZanilla" or "Jamaica." In her religious poems, the word "Sacrament" stands for the same. This imaginative drunkenness is a real communion for the poet. This vision is fleeting, and when it goes away, it is replaced by ordinary experiences of the poet. Now the mind is not a circumference, but a centre, and the circumference is an indifferent God or Nature, "Nature in his monstrous house", as we have already observed. And this gives rise to frequent moments of religious crisis in her poetry :

My Brain—begun to laugh—
I mumbled—like a fool—
And tho' 'tis Years ago—that Day—
My Brain keeps giggling—still.

And something's odd—within—
That person that I was—
And this One—do not feel the same—
Could it be Madness—this? (J. 410)

This is a state of those evenings of the brain in which the body, instead of being a circumference incorporating the experiences, becomes a "magic prison," closed against all intimations of immortality :

The Rumor's Gate was shut so tight
Before my mind was sown,
Not even a Prognostic's Push
Could make a Dent thereon— (J. 1576)

Like Blake, Emily Dickinson shows two paradoxical states of the human soul : a vision of innocence and a vision of experience. One is a vision of "Presence" and the other of "Place:"

At Half past Seven, Element
Nor Implement, be seen—
And Place was where the Presence was
Circumference between. (J. 1084)

In one the basic experience of life is partnership; in the other it is parting. Emily Dickinson's metaphors for these two states are Summer and Winter, usually; day and night, rarely:

There came a Day at Summer's full,
Entirely for me—
I thought that such were for the Saints,
Where Resurrections—be—

The Sun, as common, went abroad,
The flowers, accustomed, blew,
As if no soul the solstice passed
That maketh all things new— (J. 322)

Her "summer sister seraph" lives in the paradisal world as compared to herself, the "dark-sister," a "Druid." The spirit of winter, frost, and north, waits for the birds to come back and tell her of the sunnier world beyond. Hence equinoxes are, for her, important periods of the year. The March, a time for birds to return, when the white shell of snow will be broken and it will become colorful, or the moments in late summer when nature is made livelier by joining hands with invisible autumn.

As we have observed, Emily Dickinson's imagery is pre-eminently a pictorial imagery, and like an impressionist in art, she creates her pictures by color, rather than by outline. Purple, with its various synonyms like "Iodine," "Tyrion" and "Anethyst," is very common with her as a color of "morning" and "triumph." It becomes a symbol of the junction between life and death:

God made a little Gentian—
It tried—to be a Rose—
And failed—all the Summer laughed—
But just before the Snows—

There rose a Purple creature
That ravished all the Hill—
And Summer hid her Forehead—
And Mockery—was still—

The Frosts were her condition—
The Tyrian would not come
Until the North—invoke it—
Creator—Shall I—bloom? (J. 442).

The Paradise of the poet's consciousness, though vanishes and leaves behind moments of stupor and despair, is still survived by a light with which she can live the rest of her life without further struggle :

Why bliss so scantily disburse
Why Paradise defer—
Why Floods be served to us—in—Bowles—
I Speculate no more—(J. 756)

But, as already observed, her poetic moods are very inconsistent and unpremeditated. There are also sudden shifts from one mood to the other. In poems like "Why do they shut Me out of Heaven ?" and "If I'm lost now," her lament at the loss of vision is genuine, and the poet really feels anguished and tortured. We should not call it inconsistency. She, as a poet, speaks in different moods, voices, and tones, and creates possible imaginative and verbal response to the central unresolved problem of here and hereafter. The fact that her vision is transient makes it more flamboyant, and intensifies poet's relationship with it.

Emily Dickinson is basically a poet of the positive virtues like faith, hope, and love, which ultimately mean for her, union and peace. But in her poetry they also incorporate a great deal of opposite, that means seclusion, and renunciation. Likewise, hope is the thinnest crust of ice over despair ;

Could Hope inspect her Basis
Her Craft were done—
Has a fictitious Character
Or it has none— (J. 1283).

A Puritan to the last, she had no hope that her righteousness would help God in recognising her. She perpetually doubted at the final moment of her death that she will be thrown out of heaven. Her own vision of heaven does not guarantee an existence of heaven, though she has nowhere else to go. In keeping up with her Puritan faith, she even doubted that the life-spirit in her will end with her death. The obscure and oblique mental condition of the persona is expressed in the tone of poems like: "Doubt Me! My Dim Companion!" (J. 275) and "Struck, was I, not yet by Lightning."—(J. 925). She feels if Jesus does not recognize her in the end, she will be claimed by the dark spirit, which will recognize her as its child. Some of her poems lead us to the very edge of hell:

> Besides the deepest Cellar
> That ever Mason laid
> Look to it by its Fathoms
> Ourselves be not pursued—

and the last two lines will read:

> Leave me not ever there alone
> Oh thou Almighty God! —(J. 1182)

But for a poet with Dickinson's imagination, even the experience of Hell has got a constructive place and function. Its presence in fact may be the basis of vision itself, because, for her, "Unknown" is the biggest need of the intellect, and "Could we see all we hope—there would be madness near."

Two Biblical characters, Enoch and Elijah, attracted Emily Dickinson's imagination (probably because they were taken to the Heaven alive), and she has a poem on them:

> Elijah's Wagon knew no thill
> Was innocent of wheel
> Elijah's horses as unique
> As was his vehicle—
>
> Elijah's journey to portray
> Expire with him the skill
> Who justified Elijah
> In feats inscrutable— (J. 1254).

Dickinson had a respectful feeling for these prophets. The figure of Moses in the Bible makes her imagination more vulnerable. With Promised Land on the one hand and dark adumbration of death on the other, Moses stands on the mountain top :

It always felt to me—a wrong
To that Old Moses—done—
To let him see—the Canaan—
Without the entering—

And tho' in soberer moments—
No Moses there can be
I'm satisfied—the Romance
In point of injury—

Surpasses sharper stated—
Of Stephen—or of Paul—
For these—were only put to death—
While God's adroiter will

On Moses—seemed to fasten
With tantalizing Play
As Boy—should deal with lesser Boy—
To prove ability.

The fault—was doubtless Israel's—
Myself—had banned the Tribes—
And ushered Grand Old Moses
In Pentateuchal Robes

Upon the Broad Possession
'Twas little—He should see—
Old Man on Nebo ! Late as this —
My justice bleeds—for Thee ! (J. 597)

What establishes points of identity between Emily and Moses is the fact that Moses failed to cross the Canaan and thereby could not enter into the Promised Land, Israel. This meant that Moses, in spite of his being devout, was not able to merge his identity in God the transcendent. Emily's non-conformism on the one hand, and her desire to supplement the present world by undergoing a transformation in her consciousness on the other, place her in a direct emotional and metempiric relationship with Moses.

CHAPTER V

A Non-Conformist Poet

I

The most remarkable feature of Emily Dickinson's poetic personality is her non-conformist relation to the nonconformist faith in which she had been reared up. Her ancestor Nathaniel Dickinson sailed the Atlantic in 1630 to arrive in America in search of religious independence. Since then the non-conformism of the Puritans has passed through several phases. Her parents were Trinitarian congregationalists, as opposed to the Unitarians of the eighteenth and early nineteenth century. Their standards of thought and conduct were those of the Calvinistic Puritans. Her father's faith underwent a crisis and was finally renewed. It was natural for Emily to receive his heritage. She reflects a non-conformist personality as the speaker in her poems.

Thinking of Emily's latent rebellious spirit, the image of Huckleberry Finn naturally comes to mind. He as the protagonist of fiction had been created by Mark Twain only ten years before Emily was dead. The impact of civilization and environment on the growing personalities of Emily Dickinson and Huck Finn, is similar. Huck Finn, the naughty boy, provides parallels to Emily Dickinson's non-conformist attitude to faith, an attitude which is of utmost importance in understanding her poetry. Her poetic outpourings are a brilliant record of the spiritual pains and pleasures she experienced in the process of disregarding the doctrines and discarding the conventionally accepted Christian God and dogma. She became rebellious by deliberate and conscious choice, and thereby became saturated with the spirit of non-conformity. She grew up in a Christian family but she discovered soon that she was not a devout. She did not possess a talent for conviction in the accepted dogma. In her life, as in her poetry, she always brought an interrogative attitude to the doctrinal aspects of Christianity.

Nothing clarifies and illumines our understanding of the poetic personality of Emily Dickinson so much as a comparison with Mark Twain's mental child Huck Finn, who sets the highest value on truth. Truth is the whole of Huck's conscious demand upon the world of adults, as it is with Emily. He is never convinced of the values set over against him by society, and he continues to believe that the adult world has planned an everlasting conspiracy to lie to him. Both Huck and Emily set over against the dogma the norms of experience discovered through an arrogant passion for truth. "Truth is so rare a thing, it is delightfull to tell it," she once wrote to Higginson while sending him her poems for scrutiny. Huck and Emily, cut off from dogmatic moorings, keep afloat in search of truth much in the way Emerson recommends in his essay "Intellect" :

> God offers to every mind its choice between truth and repose. Take which you please,—You can never have both. Between these, as a pendulum, man oscillates. He in whom the love of repose predominates will accept the first creed, the first philosophy, the first political party he meets,—most likely his father's... He in whom the love of truth predominates will keep himself aloof from all mooring, and afloat.[1]

In both, love of repose is outgrown by love of truth and hence the first creed, the first philosophy they encounter, meets with their subsequent rejection of it.

Even the apparent differences between Emily and Huck finally lead to the most significant parallelisms. Emily may not be as simple and innocent as Huck : she was brought up in an highly intellectualized and sophisticated family and lived in an academic atmosphere as both her grandfather and father were leading educationists of their day. She went to school at Amherst academy, and studied there Latin, French,

[1]Quoted in Hyatt H. Waggoner, *American Poets: From the Puritans to the Present*, p. 187.

history, rhetoric, botany and mental philosophy. Huck, on the other hand, taken over by widow Douglas to civilize him, feels rough, uneasy and dismal at the regular and decent ways of the widow. He hates the school and can hardly stand it. Moreover, we do not have any image of Huck beyond his boyhood, as we do not have that of Emily prior to her maturity, or whatever of Emily as a girl we have is mostly conjectural. As a poet, her Muse was set to work at a considerably grown up age, her Minerva having been born full-dressed. Excepting half a dozen occasional verses, there is not a single scrap of poetry that can be dated earlier than 1858,[2] whereas *Huck writes his novel when a boy.* But we must note that from her very childhood, she shunned all social distractions and the habit of increasing an intense sequestration, requiring no scrumble on her part, made her able to say throughout her life what she had said at the age of sixteen: "I don't know anything more about affairs in the world than if I was in a trance."

Again, Emily has persistently used, in her poems, the mask of a child, and a naughty one at that, while acting before God in the great drama of poetic creation :

God is indeed a Jealous God—
He cannot bear to see
That we had rather not with Him
But with each other play. (J. 1719).

Such a childlike simplicity was a part of Emily's personality. In his first interview with Emily, Higginson was struck by her childlike simplicity. In April 1853, when she was in her twenty-third year, Emily wrote to her brother Austin: "I wish we were children now. I wish we were *always* children, how to grow up I dont know." To grow up meant to her to leave the clan. She was tied very closely with her little cousins even at a grown up age. A part of nature persisted in the game of "little girlhood."

[2]T.H. Johnson, ed., *The Poems of Emily Dickinson* (Harvard University Press, 1963), p. XIX.

Huck travels extensively, but Emily deliberately retires to her father's garden to lead a remote life with the bees and bobolinks and flowers of it. But, nevertheless, both seek a withdrawal from society: Emily shuts her doors and allows no one to obtrude; Huck, away from society, enjoys the invulnerable peace on the river shore and the raft. At the opening of chapter nineteen, Huck is afraid lest the peace of the daybreak should be disturbed by any intrusion, that is by contact with social order. Both have the adventurous and playful spirit and try to satisfy it to the maximum, although their ways are different. Huck has all the possible experiences of a river life, and Emily travelled widely in the imaginative realm of human experience. Emily realized the Emersonian self possession to the extreme. The doctrine of the supremacy of the individual had a great charm for her. She took a close picturesque view of her internal possibilities, and found in the landscape of her soul, all sorts of sunrise and moonlight effects. Huck experienced them on the rivershore. In the mode of her life as in the spirit of her poetry, Emily carried out the doctrine of self-sufficient individualism to its apogee.

Huck's instinctive humanity is open to every reader of the novel. One of the characteristic features of *Huckleberry Finn* is the gradual development of Huck's character, his growth in social awareness. At a moment of awareness and commitment Huck shouts "They're after us" and makes a common cause with Jim. The quest for Jim's freedom which Huck undertakes becomes the main instrument of his growth. He is so intensely involved in the social cause of Jim's liberation that he prefers damnation in hell to getting a place in heaven. Even when he learns that there is an award for Jim, he is not tempted by money. He is pulled one way by his traditions and environment and another way by his instinctive humanitarianism. He realises that the journey would be a failure unless it took Jim to freedom, though journey was not the means by which Jim obtained freedom. It only took him towards the land of slavery. At the end of the book we discover that Jim had been free for two months, that his freedom had been granted by old Miss Watson. On the whole, it may be said that Huck struggles with important social issues.

Nothing like Huck's involvement in the social problem of slavery can be said of Emily. She appears, rather, notoriously aloof from the contemporary social and political life. "When the civil war was beginning to force on America the troubled vision of its revolutionary destiny," observes Northrop Frye, "Emily Dickinson retired to her garden to remain, like Wordsworth's skylark, within kindred points of heaven and home."[3] Like Blake, with whom she has been compared ever since the first publication (1890) of her poems, or in modern times like Wallace Stevens, Emily has a persistent concern with the reality of the poetic vision, a reality which is the offspring of the creative imagination, and not a reflection of the objective world. But not even a small particle of Blake's social vision can be found in Emily. Blake is pre-eminently a humanitarian poet, concerned, *inter alia*, with the problems of child labour, Negro Slavery, and prostitution.

In spite of her withdrawal from social upheavals of the time, the curious fact remains that the years of Emily's greatest poetic outburst were exactly those of the civil war in America (1861-1865) fought over the issue of slavery. This correlation between national crisis and flood of poetic energy may not be a matter of sheer accident. Although the Civil War seemed to her "oblique" and outside her orbit, her sensibility could not remain unaffected by that decisive and epoch-making incident in the history of America. Writing to her cousins about the death and burial of the first Amherst casualty, she says :

> "Sorrow seems more general than it did, and not the estate of a few persons, since the war began; and if the anguish of others helped one with one's own, now would be many medicines."[4]

Besides, such poems as the following bring Emily close to Huck :

---

[3]Northrop Frye, *Fables of Identity*, pp. 216-217.

[4]Quoted in James Reeves, *Commitment to Poetry* (London, 1969), p. 186.

If I can stop one Heart from breaking
I shall not live in vain
If I can ease one Life the Aching
Or cool one Pain.

Or help one fainting Robin
Unto his Nest again
I shall not live in Vain. (J. 919).

With all her seclusion, she loved the world: "I have perfect confidence in God and his promises and yet I know not why, I feel that the world holds a predominant place in my affections." Where a choice is to be made between God and man, she will choose man discarding religious faith as an enforced choice. Emily did not erect an ivory tower for herself. Huck glorified a Negro slave; Emily glorified Man.

Not the least remarkable thing about both these persons is that their sympathy is quick and immediate, though never sentimental. In spite of their profound and bitter knowledge of human deprivation they never shrink from being a friend to man. Huck alone feels miserable at the so-called drunken man who endeavours to ride the horse when the entire range of circus audience laughs at him. Emily, though most often in quarrel with the world on religious doctrines, clears away her heart by saying that her poems are her letters to the world.

Both Huck and Emily project certain archetypal patterns of non-conformist ideals in the nineteenth century America, and our criticism will be directed towards what they stand and long for, not towards what they have achieved. Their stories tell the lives lived, as also lives suppressed—a fine combination of experience and wish.

II

Emily became alomst an epicure in sorting out a balance between experience and wish. She could satisfy her wish in imagination against what experience apparently procured for her. Her own perception of life and her vision of it were the only things which she felt to be concerned with. Experience manifested itself in knowledge, and wish in vision. It was this individualistic perception which impelled her on the path of non-conformity.

A searching glance at Emily's letters reveals the workings of the meditative mind of a devotional poet, pouring out innumerable poems crowded with Biblical allusions. She has, however, her own definitive attitude towards things which is omnipresent in her poetry with vicissitudes of tone. She has a circumference of non-conformity with a centre of whatever comes her way. Never does she cross the boundaries of this circumference, not even when her Muse is set free to make an idiosyncratic display of her spiritual longings with complete freedom from reticence. Non-conformity is, with her, a perennial artistic device.

Both Emily and Huck, as literary personalities, are symbols of discontent against institutionalism. Emily fulminated against religion, Huck against civilization and slavery. The moral perceptions of both are determined by their respective families, by the early environment in which they have been reared up. In other words, they have both got a very deep introduction to conformity before they break loose from it and yield to non-conformity.

Emily's was a deeply religious family. But her sincerity regarding religious matters was several times put to question, with the result that J.L. Jenkins, the local Congregational minister, was arranged by Edward Dickinson to offer her some spiritual guidance. But the report came out to the perplexed parents that she was "sound." She remained a critic of Puritan God throughout her life, though she would have been, nothing, she feels, without God. The reverence she had for her religious heritage is made clear in a sampler she embroidered when she was fifteen :

Jesus permit thy Gracious Name to stand
As the first effort of an infant's hand.

It ends with the plea that Jesus may write His name upon her heart, just as she has embroidered it on the sampler. In spite of such statements as "I do not respect doctrines," there are times when she longs for faith, like a child :

Those—dying then,
Knew where they went—
They went to God's Right Hand—
That Hand is amputated now
And God cannot be found—

The abdication of Belief
Makes the Behaviour small—
Better an ignis fatuus
Than no illume at all— (J. 1551)

Huck's respect for doctrines may be illustrated by his relations with Tom and Jim. Tom would not do anything against the rules laid down in the books. When Ben Rogers, a member of their Gang, wants to know what being "ransomed" means, Tom replies thus :

"I don't know. But that's what they do.
I've seen it in books ; and so of course
that's what we've got to do."

"But how can we do it if don't wc know what it is?

"Why, blame it all, we've got to do it. Don't I tell
you it's in the books? Do you want to go to doing
different from what's in the books, and get things all
muddled up?"[5]

Similarly, Jim will always act in the light of the fears stemming from his conventionally derived charms and superstitions, Huck is by his very nature free from such institutionalism. But when he is in the company of Tom, he clings to the bookish rules : Jim's taboos are also respected by him, especially after the rattlesnake skin incident. Thus, as in Emily's case, most of his moral perceptions are inherited from the influences around him.

---

[5]Mark Twain, *The Adventures of Huckleberry Finn*, ed., Lionel Trill. ing (New York, 1953), p. 9. All quotations from *Huckleberry Finn* refer to this edition, unless indicated otherwise.

In Chapter VIII Huck agrees not to report that Jim has run away. But the influence of his upbringing comes over when he accepts that "People would call me a low-down Abolitionist and despise me for keeping mum...." Even at a very advanced stage in the book, Huck's sense of right and wrong, as bestowed upon him by his family, has not been diminished. In chapter XVI, he clearly manifests his conventionally derived moral perception :

> "What had poor Miss Watson done to you that you could see her nigger go off right under your eyes and never say one single word? What did that poor old woman do to you that you could treat her so mean? Why, she tried to learn you your book, she tried to learn you your manners, (she tried to learn you to be Christian) she tried to be good to you...."[6]

Both Huck and Emily apparently have a kind of reverence for orthodox religion and morality. So, the important question is, what makes them act otherwise. What makes Huck capable of mistakes in perception and judgement, troubled by doubts and conflicting impulses ? What makes Emily say "I do not respect doctrines?" Such questions naturally lead us to the philosophical views of Hobbes, Bentham, Mill, Locke, and their group. A summary version of their views on the point is that the only possible motive to any action is always a desire to avoid pain and obtain happiness. The only reason behind the performance of good actions is to acquire the greatest amount of happiness.

This philosophy has got some universality in its implication. Emily and Huck are always conscious of their "delinquencies" when they do or think something unconventional. But doing wrong, for them, is the only source of acquiring the greatest amount of happiness. They acknowledge the traditional virtues, but upbraid themselves for being uncomfortable with them. Huck says : "Well, then, says I, what's the use you learning to do right when it's troublesome to do right and ain't no trouble to do wrong, and the wages is the same?" Note here, "it's troublesome to do right." Huck's questionings remind us of Emily's letter which she

[6] *Ibid.*, p. 88.

wrote to Jane Humphrey on the 23rd January, 1850: "The path of duty looks very ugly indeed—and the place where I want to go more amiable—a great deal—it is so much easier to do wrong than right—so much pleasanter to be evil than good."

And here we see very clearly Ernest Hemingway's definition of morality, as we find appearing early in *Death in the Afternoon*: "I know only that what is moral is what you feel good after." One of his characters in *The Sun Also Rises*, Brett Ashley, says much the same thing. According to this code, Emily and Huck test the ethics of an action by the way they feel after it is done. Thereby they become unconscious followers of the Eudaemonistic philosophy of life which makes happiness the test of rectitude. It would not be an exaggeration if we say they believe in doing wrong for the sake of it.

Another reason of their non-conformity may, of course, be attributed to their keen sensibility which probingly penetrates whatever is within its reach. When Huck says he will go to hell, he is imaginatively there. When Miss Watson lectures to him about the advantages of prayer and the Bible, he raises awkward questions regarding religion and its promises: "She told me to pray, everyday, and whatever I asked for I would get it. But it wasn't so. I tried it." Huck sets over experience against dogma. Similarly, when Emily's emotions take a religious turn, as they often do, she does not allow to be curbed by the discipline of belief. Her sensibility, like that of Huck, is wilful. She can believe a thing only if it makes a direct appeal to her experience, including imaginative experience. She wrote to Higginson about her family: "They are all religious—except me—and address an Eclipse every morning—whom they call their Father." Both Emily and Huck have got a passion for truth. It is this passion that inspires Huck to attack prayer and enables Emily to call her family's God an "Eclipse."

Another, and a very important, cause of their latent rebellious spirit which works like a torch-bearer in their conduct, is their imperfect upbringing. When Huck's own conscience pricks him for not giving up the runaway slave, he finds out an excuse for himself on the ground of his early environment and its influences :

> ...I knowed very well I had done wrong, and I see it warn't no use for me to try to learn to do right : a body that don't get started right when he's little ain't got no show—when the pinch comes to there ain't nothing to back him up."

Huck, who has got a drunken father and no mother, perpetually faces many problems which always remain unanswered and this avowedly makes him a problem child of the kind he is.

Emily's case is not very different from that of Huck, although she has got both her mother and father. If we study her relationship with her parents, in the light of the statements she makes now and then to her family members or to her friends and so called "preceptors," we can see that there were many missing links, and thereby making it difficult for her to feel a normal attachment with her parents. Her father was very much like Elizabeth Barrett's father. But Emily proved to be less obdurate and more submissive than Elizabeth. At times she got so much scared of her father that she confused him with God. She once remarked to Higginson that her mother "did not care for thought" and her father was "too busy to notice what we do." This lack of intimate and educationally profitable relationship with her parents naturally led her to choose a way of her own and evolve her own code of judging things.

John Cody, in his book *The inner Life of Emily Dickinson* (1971), suggests that Emily Dickinson's troubles began not with her father she feared and loved but with her neurotic, inadequate mother. No other circumstance in Emily's life can have had as profound an effect on her as those unhappy early transactions in the Dickinson nursery. Cody emphasizes that all the psychological, social, and religious troubles which Emily had to undergo are ultimately traceable to the psychological determinations rooted in her transactions with her mother. There may be some paucity and exaggeration in this hard judgement, but the fact that she was never close to her mother is beyond doubt. She once remarked that she had no mother, she did not know what a mother was. This inadequacy on the part of her mother surely accounts to make her incapable of assenting to doctrine.

In spite of a great reverence for orthodox religion and morality Emily and Huck do not feel that the path of social conformity is their path. It does not, however, make them indifferent to the questions of dogmas. By his dislike of civilization, Huckleberry Finn is involved in civilization upto his ears. The more he rejects society, the more does he get involved with it. As for Emily, a remark made in 1848 is revealing :

> "There is a great deal of religious interest here and many are flocking to the ark of safety. I have not yet given up to the claims of Christ, but trust I am not entirely thoughtless on so important a subject."

Instead of making any final acceptance or rejection, Emily and Huck prefer to struggle with their faith.

Non-conformity is a blind force which drives but does not direct. The inevitable result is a wrestle with the conscience. The intensity of this conflict owes much to the fact that they have a deep concern with the things which they apparently seem to be unconcerned with. Emily's family exhibited all the outstanding traits of religious orthodoxy, as did Miss Watson of a valley society. All the polite lies of civilization that suffocate Huck's spirit are spoken by Miss Watson. The essential conflict is between Huck's and Emily's aspiration on the one hand and the conventional codes for which their respective families are spokesmen on the other.

Paine, one of Mark Twain's distinguished biographers, suggested that Huck's struggle is a psychological struggle—between conscience and law on one side, and sympathy on the other. He has got a very active and brisk mind which cannot be put to rest. He is always in a conflict. He decides to protect the slave, although it involves going wicked and suffering eternal punishment hereafter. He abandons the values of society and decides to go outside its ways. When he hears that Jim's discovery is attached with some award, money offers him no temptation. But when he is invaded by conscience he goes so far as to write a note to Miss Watson, Jim's owner. He feels satisfied at the time :

> ...thinking how near I come to being lost and going to hell....
>
> ..but afterward-... I was a trembling, because I'd got to decide, forever, betwixt two things, and I knowed it. I studied a minute, sort of holding my breath, and then says to myself:
>
> "All right, then, I'll go to hell"—and tear it up.

Thus in his struggle with his "yaller-dog" conscience, Huck comes over it and vindicates the realities of friendship, loyalty, and courage.

Emily had received a very clear cut notion of religious orthodoxy, her father being one of the chief pillars of Amherst society. One was considered religious in that village society, if one experienced a conviction of salvation, became an active member of the church, and publicly professed faith in its dogmas. To be uncertain of any of the dogmas was to give proof that one was not one of the saints, the Elect, who would be saved. In the beginning Emily was uncertain that she could believe the dogmas, in the end she was certain that she could not. Her poem, "I heard a fly buzz when I died" gives a prevision of death with suggestions of damnation. In this poem Emily speaks through the voice of a person already dead and damned. The first two stanzas and a half wonderfully wrap up in sensuous images the idea of dying, with suggestions of salvation—"When the King/Be witnessed—in the Room. The "King" is the Savior, Christ, who has come to redeem the dead. But then something else happens: "There interposed a Fly—With Blue." The Blue Flye Satan, the Prince of Darkness, comes to claim the soul of the dead. And his claims gain priority. The poem uses the Puritan dogma to assess Emily's ultimate fate in an ironic way. I say "ironic" because there is a tension between what the poem "states" and what it implies. The implication is that the dogma is fraught with the dangers of self-righteousness, and an honest acceptance of the human condition is preferable.

Emily declared herself "standing alone in rebellion, and growing very careless." She refused to listen to Mrs. Steele, who preached upon "predestination." She resisted the threats implicit in her religious heritage with such irresistible charm and delicacy, yet firmness, that it is very difficult to decide when she has a delightful intimacy and when a subjective privation with the Supreme Rules of the Universe :

It was too late for Man—
But early, yet, for God—
Creation—impotent to help—
But Prayer—remained—our Side—

How excellent the Heaven—
When Earth—cannot be had—
How hospitable—then—the face
Of our Old Neighbor—God— (J. 623).

In this poem, apparently written in a playful mood, the persona is in fact under a deep religious crisis, willing to find God's 'Right Hand', but not capable of total renunciation of the earth. The tone of the poem is steeped in irony and paradox. The sense of guilt is evident, but the feeling of surrender is lacking. 'Man' realizes very late that this ultimate asylum is God's abode, Heaven : yet God is too willing to help man and respond to his prayer.

This poem, if understood in the light of its tone and speaker's attitude toward the situation, sums up in as few words as possible Emily's religious attitude.

Dickinson's recusancy to the generally accepted creed of New England, and her predisposition to Catholic thought, her exaltation of death and her informality with Divinity bring her in link with G. M. Hopkins, "the Phoenix among the Jesuits," as Dickinson was a phoenix among the Puritans. Under the aegis of their non-conformism, both these poets had departed from the orthodox structures of form in verse. Hopkins made a verse outmoded in his Victorian England but signalized in our day in its character of natural harmony of sprung rhythm. Emily is his worthy ancestor of verse liberties.

The essential conflict is between what Huck and Emily think they stand for and what social and family pressures force them to do. Huck knows well what he feels about Jim; Emily knows what she feels about religion : but they also know what they are expected to do in these matters. This division within their mind corresponds to another characteristic quality of their personality—namely, a constant inconsistency in their behaviour. In this sense, they are opportunists: they do whatever seems to be handiest at the time. Their non-conformity is born out of their intensely moving honesty.

A moody poet as Emily is, she always gives herself to the moment. Many of her pronouncements are more occasional than definitive. Her sincerity is beyond question, but it only leads her to accept whatever would help her at the given occasion. In one of her poems, "How brittle are the Piers" (J. 1433), she urges that we may still believe in God and His promises, the evidence being Christ's Word. This poem was written to console Higginson on the death of his wife. She also wrote to Higginson that to be human is more than to be divine, for when Christ was divine He was uncontended till He became human. Such sudden changes and inconsistency of ideas can frequently be encountered in Emily Dickinson.

Even Huck is not an exemption here. This aspect of Huck's nature is illustrated in chapter XII when he invades a farm to "borrow" a melon, corn or other provisions.

> "Pap, always said it wasn't to harm to borrow things if you was meaning to pay them back some time : but the widow said it warn't anything but a soft name for stealing, and no decent body would do it."

Taking heed of the widow, Jim and Huck decide "to pick out two or three things from the list and say" "we won't borrow them any more," and award immunity to crabapples and persimmons. "I was glad the way it come out," says Huck, "because crabapples ain't ever good, and the p'simmons wouldn't be ripe for two or three months yet." It is a neat instance of Huck's being an opportunist in matters of daily ethics as Emily is in matters of faith. The essential mental processes involved in both the cases are the same. Emerson, whom Emily admired, wrote that one should not be afraid of contradicting oneself : and Whitman, whom she disliked, said much the same thing—"Do I contradict myself?/ Very well then I contradict myself". I connect Huck's and Emily's non-conformism and contradictions with their honest opportunism of religious and moral perceptions.

Emily's deep concern with religious affairs is obvious. As for Huck, the germs of Dickinsonian religious non-conformity are explicit in his nature. We see him every now and then probing the problems of religion and its promises. The first manifestation of his non-conformist nature is to be found in the first three chapters of the book. Thus he criticizes prayer and expresses his view of heaven. Religion stands at the center of the system of values of any society, and by refuting the social values one cannot claim to be honoring the religious ones. The most vital and crucial of Huck's crises comes when his conscience, along with secular reasons, pelts him with religious threats :

> At last, when it hit me all of a sudden that there was the plain hand of Providence slapping me in the face and letting me know my wickedness was being watched all the time from up there in heaven, whilst I was stealing a poor old woman's nigger that hadn't ever done me no harm, and now was showing me there's one that's always on the lookout, and ain't a-going to allow me such miserable doings to go only just so far and no further, I most dropped in my tracks I was so scared.[7]

But getting "scared" cannot swerve him from the path he discovers through gropings and falterings. He gets over his religious crisis by following his sympathies towards human nature. He completes his breach with society, at the end of the book, by deciding to light out far the territory ahead of the rest, as Emily decides to be damned rather than conform to dogma.

III

According to Romantic philosophy every individual human personality is an organism. It requires a reconstitution of it if it has to undergo a fundamental change of any kind. Its old self "dies" and a totally new self, an unpremeditated organism, is "born." Both of the personalities discussed so far emancipate themselves from the incarceration of conventionalism and emerge in a new form under the mask of

---

[7]Mark Twain, *Writings* (Definitive Edition, New York, 1922-25), XIII, pp. 294-95.

non-conformity. In this technical process of ‘.death” and “rebirth” the original personalities which the individuals themselves cannot stand are dismantled, and the newly born personalities wrestle and flutter in void to seek a solid stand.

Emily remains occupied with the theme of death to the last, and Huck stages out the scene of his own fake-murder at the very beginning of the book. These patterns of death are not merely artistic devices, they have deeper symbolic meaning. At the time of his departure from his drunken father, Huck's staging the fake-murder of himself symbolizes, in the light of Romantic philosophy I have mentioned above, that the pressures of civilization and respectability have crushed him down to death and a new personality is going to be reborn on the river and the raft. After renouncing the conventions of his time and place, Huck goes out to adopt a morality based on New Testament ethic in the form of his duty to Jim. The river provides him a means of escape, and a place where he can test his code. “What you want above all things, on a raft,” remarks Huck, “is for everybody to be satisfied, and feel right and kind towards others.” This human credo constitutes the paramount affirmation of Huck's character and is brought by him to the river, a God that has a mind and will of its own He has already abandoned the Providence of Widow and Miss Watson. He becomes a thrall to this river-God since it appears to embody a great moral ideal for him.

Emily's rejection of orthodoxy, too, was complete. Her frequent return to the theme of death speaks out symbolically her withdrawal from one faith to another. After rejecting her father's God as an ‘Eclipse,’ she finds a wider God and in a new way asserts the claim of life after death. At this stage Emily Dickinson becomes a poet of the consciousness, and her poetry an adventuring exercise in the realms of “circumference” and imagination, where nature attains new interpretations and intimacies.

This pattern of commingling between a human personality and the river (in the case of Huck), between nature and human circumference, and above all between human consciousness and a greater circumference (in the case of Emily), is acquired after a fictitious death and an imaginary rebirth. The pattern clarifies three things. First, for saving oneself from running omok, one has to kneel down and surrender oneself before some greater and superior power. This power may be in the form of social values and the systems of society, or in the shape of legal and doctrinal religion. In more emancipated and sensitive individuals, it may exist in their own standards and codes. Personality requires some solid shelter, whether inherited from society and family or erected by the individual as his own.

Second, the fundamental realities of life have their own place and power. They cannot be denied : they have got to be accepted either one way or the other. Love and Religion—these two have got a very strong bearing on human nature. They make a continual appeal on heart which one cannot break away with. In Huck's instance there is no fundamental distinction between the river and the ideal human society, Human love and affection are the real charm of his life on the river. In Jim he finds the image of an affectionate father. He is at odds with the Christian God, with the Providence of the widow and that of Miss Watson. In the Mississippi he has got a true God—a God who, like any other god, is benign and deceptive simultaneously. He adores this God perpetually and fits himself to its ways. The God in turn fosters his goodness. Emily, after abandoning the Mosaic religion, accepts an Orphic religion in which dogmas and doctrines penetrate her sensibility like music. After finding herself as not "religious" in any sense that her family could accept, she has found for herself a new faith, a new religious experience. In her newly born faith Christ is no other than Jehovah or Cupid. Thus her non-conformism finally turns into an *experience*, rather than an *understanding* of religion.

Third, and most important, the circles of conformity and non-conformity are set rolling by the word "identity." A world is set over against us. We cannot conform ourselves to its ways and modes unless we feel an "identity" with it. Things which we watch every time, which keep us surrounding them every minute, definitely make a direct appeal to our sensibility. We have become so much accustomed to this "identity" that we are hardly conscious of it. But as soon as we find ourselves incapable of seeking an identity between our sensibility and the objects set over against it, we become non-conformists.

Alienated from society and its dogma, Huck sought an identity with life on the river : Emily, with "circumference." This identity necessarily generates conformity of a new kind, the reborn one.

CHAPTER VI

Conclusion

I

The preceding chapters of my study have scrutinized Emily Dickinson's selected poems in detail, thematically and stylistically, and have tried to go deep in discussion of the issues involved, In view of the liberty Dickinson playfully and ironically took with themes and prosody, it could not, perhaps may not, be possible, in spite of the most exhaustive study of some of her leading poems, to draw generalisations regarding her basic attitude to chosen themes, or comment upon the ideological and stylistic characteristics of her poetry. But a close and concentrated reading of the poems, which includes variant readings and choices of the text, enabled me to have a fairly balanced idea of some of the primary assumptions which, consciously or unconsciously, shaped themes as well as structures of her poems.

Emily was a staunch Puritan, though it worked the other way round, since she was laboriously antagonistic to it. Her attitude, therefore, to love, death, nature and religion befits an analytical study against a wide perspective of her age, rearing, and religious background. She was a child of Puritan New England born too late to live by the inherited formulas of Puritanism. In contrast to Whitman who inherited nothing and was free to welcome the new age with nonchalant amiability of one who has nothing to lose, Emily Dickinson faced her age and background with the desperation and ambivalence of one who feared to lose anything because of her involving and sensitive nature. Her individual struggle was an unconscious replica of the greater conflict going on elsewhere ; the acute accidents of her own life and experiences paralleled and intensified manifold the predicament (caused by Civil War) her generation was going through.

She met the realities of her life with a poet's consciousness, and worked out personal adjustments according to the patterns of her needs. That is one reason why as a careful, conscious, and deliberate choice, she became a recluse. Allen Tate was the first critic of importance who seriously attempted to chart the influence of Puritan tradition on Emily Dickinson's poetry (In *Contradictory Essays*, 1933). Then the problem was taken in right earnest by her biographers—Whicher Todd, Bingham, Johnson etc. My own observation in this regard is that the influence of Puritanism on her formal poetics has generally been overlooked, and the concern of critics has been mostly to trace its influence on her personality and way of thinking. Some critics even account Puritanism for her seclusion.

It is not important whether as an ideology she accepted or rejected Puritanism. The main point that I could discover is that Puritanism had given her a great moral, intellectual, and spiritual discipline : it was a part and parcel of her psyche, though its doctrinal aspects, she persistently rejected and remained antogonistic to. In Emily's poetry, the formulation of her symbols is directly related to her Puritan background, and the Bible gives structural and thematic images to many of her poems, some among her best, like "Because I could not stop for Death.".

Literature gives us an experience of the heights and depths the human mind can conceive, which analogically correspond to the concepts of "heaven" and "hell" in religion. In Emily Dickinson's case, it is difficult to realize the poignancy and intensity of her religious experience. The theme of "death", which is central to her poetry, has been taken from the world of religion. Frequent references from Revelation and Corinthians in the Bible clustered her imagination in her poems on death. Death is closed inside the prisms of the human mind, and the sense of primordial human vision and embryonic emotion, radiating from death, gives it a poetic magic. Her death consciousness takes her not only outside her life, but also outside the time she is living in :

> Behind me dips Eternity,
> Before me Immortality,
> Myself the term between—

My study and investigations have aimed at suggesting a discerning and centripetal approach to Emily Dickinson's poetry, with poems at the center. Published scholarship on Emily Dickinson provides one with innumerable insights, some indeed rare and precious, the major part of it has sadly failed to give the prudent attention and observation her poetry deserves. While critics have been busy trying to give shape to Emily's "amorphous" life in an attempt to measure its length and width, their sense for an appreciation of her poetry has remained immured and impeded.

The biographical and psychological approaches to Emily Dickinson's poetry (as, for instance, those of John Cody and John Walsh) have failed to realize that in Emily's poetry, the distinction between the poet and the "persona", or the "poetic voice" is very important and evident. Emily herself warned her readers that "when I state myself as the representative of my verse—it does not mean—me—but a supposed person." Analyzed in this light, Emily Dickinson's poetry is never a "self-expression" as many critics have assumed.

The verbal personality or the speaking voice as it emerges from Dickinson's poetry is that of a poet speaking in many voices and with many masks. The morbid concern of one poem is contradicted by the humorous irony of the other. A careful inspection finally reveals that no single poem may be an example either of the controlling idea behind her themes or of the mode of expression employed therein. In order to form a definite view about Emily Dickinson's poetry, therefore, we must understand it as a whole, in the totality of its visions, perceptions, intonations, and symbols.

The "principle of decorum" (George T. Wright's phrase) does not apparently apply to Emily Dickinson's poetry, because she neither caters to the limitations imposed by the literary conventions of the age, nor to the discipline set by the language of literature. She has her roots in the turbulent orginality of purpose, unable any longer to accept the traditional modes of life and thought. She struggles throughout to create a new *world-order*. Dickinson's independence allowed her to assay experience directly, avoiding in her most powerful poems the decorous gestures of easy faith and language, as, for example, prescribed to her by her "preceptor" friend T.W. Higginson. The poems in their honesty, as rightly observed by Allen Tate, are "almost obscene."

One of the intractable problems about Emily Dickinson is that we do not have a full theoretical background of her poetry, and her random utterances here and there are not more than stray and impressionistic reflections. Among major American poets, she helps us the least, because she has left no extended interpretative discourse. After a close reading of her poetry we are not at all surprised at her seemingly contradictory beliefs about religion and other metaphysical problems. Reality for her took shape most fully in her fictive arrangements : she called the poetic consciousness that presided over her creative acts, "Uncle Emily's Ardor for the lie" (L-II—315).

Dickinson's lyrics are mostly dramatic in nature, and reflect different moods and emotions, not always corresponding to each other. But an attitude consistent all through her poetry is one of uncompromise and dissipation. There is, in her poetry, invariably an element of spiritual crisis and a subsequent struggle to step out of it. But every time after reaching the brink of solution, the poet, by choice, likes to come back to the original state of conflict, as, for instance, in the poem "I years had been from Home."

Perhaps this battle within lends magnificence, exuberance, and dynamism to Emily Dickinson's poetry. It gives such a sensational urgency to the poet's life that mostly she is ecstatic, and writes poetry like an inspired oracle. We hear strange stories of her ecstatic moods. Poetry here gets lifted up to the mythical plane, and, instead of being the verbal representation of an experience, it becomes the experience itself. The poet, while singing about an object, often considers herself to be singing as one : "I would not paint—a picture—/I'd rather be the One/ I would not talk, like Cornets —/ I'd rather be the One/ Nor would I be a Poet—/ It's finer —own the Ear—/ Enamored—impatient—content—(J. 505), and finally the poet wishes to have the art to stun herself with "Bolts of Melody." That may partly explain why Emily Dickinson has got a preference for oracular, associative rhythm (in Northrop Frye's sense of the term) as a technique in her poetry.

It is a generic characteristic of lyric poetry to "turn its back" on the reader (that is one reason why while writing her poems, Emily had some very selective audience in her mind, and the ghost of publication never haunted her). Since Emily Dickinson's lyrics represent the drama of her inner conflict, they are many times in the form of a dialogue or an interaction between her spirit and a situation with emotions and characters set into it. Hence her lyrics consist of a number of internal characters, or dramatic voices. In order to maintain the decorum or the appropriateness of style, she chooses voices, moods, and images which are in tune with the emotion of the situation. In such poems, the rhythm is usually conversational, as in "I died for Beauty—but was scarce/ Adjusted in the Tomb"— (J. 449).

After Blake, Emily Dickinson is the only major poet who could tackle conversational rhythm in verse so successfully that it became real poetry. In the poem just mentioned, a strict adherence to short metre (8, 6, 8, 6)lends an epigrammatic accuracy to the conversational rhythm. A full-fledged dialogue in question-answer form is well fitted into the eight-six-eight-six rhythmical beat. On the contrary, in other poems, the loosening of stanzaic pattern is not due to carelessness, or her lack of mastery over the mode. It is to give sharpness and urgency to the emotion and the poetic thought which the poet wishes to communicate, and thereby to make the lyric rhythm more precise. Her deliberate liberty with many conventional devices makes her associative-oracular-rhythm more compressed and quickly graspable.

In some recent studies, Emily Dickinson has variously been described as a transcendentalist, metaphysical, romantic, and more lately, even a confessional, and an existentialist poet.

The area of her poetry yields to the above but exceeds them in its thematic range. As far as the romantic quality of her poetry is concerned, if romanticism means the ability to wonder and to reflect, the search for the meaning of the unknown, to understand the present moment in terms of past and future, the ability to fear, doubt and be amazed, Emily Dickinson unquestionably has these qualities in abundance. When reason and religious authority both failed her, she found her asylum in the strictures of these larger emotions, and centralized her entire poetic drama around them.

Emily had something oriental in the very manner of her existence. Her need for a preceptor, use of witty and brief poems as a means of communication, and most importantly, her seclusion, all these have a typical oriental touch in them. Even otherwise, she was highly selective in her human relations and avoided all that seemed to threaten the balance of her deliberately obliterated life. As a creative writer, her nuances of awareness were subtle, delicate, and mysterious. Her perceptions were so immediate, and sharp that for her, mere sense of living was joy enough. It gave her a feeling of transport and transcendence. She used to be so much entangled with the intensity of her poetic consciousness that it required her all staying at one place to keep running. In this respect Emily Dickinson's poetry is essentially a poetry of consciousness, in which her poetic mind passes from one world to another, and is often simultaneously aware of both. The poet stays where she is, and it is the poetry which travels. In the poem "I never saw a Moor" (J. 1052), the poet is sure of the spot where heaven is, though she admits that she has not visited it, and she knows how the heather looks and what a billow is, though she has neither seen a moor nor the sea.

Emily Dickinson's approach to nature is refreshingly new, having the bees, wind, birds, bobolinks, butterflies, flowers, the cycle of seasons, and the sun inside the circumference of her consciousness. All these nature objects are implanted inside her mind.[9] As Emily matures as a poet, the physical presence of the humming bird in her garden (1862) becomes a mere sensation of "a route of evanescence" (1878) ; the "sunsets" she can have in "a cup"; and she can reckon how many notes there are in "new Robin's extasy": or Bee, "the Debauchee of Dew," partakes how many cups for her intoxication. At the religious level, her imagination attains a propensity to project itself as the religion of consciousness. This poet's sensations, at this plane too, attain a clairvoyance and a vision which is quick and encompassing, but transitory. This vision comes and goes unpredictably, and finally disappears as death. For each of this "ecstatic instant," in quivering ratio to the ecstasy" an anguish is to be paid (J. 125). When this vision ceases finally, it is like the "distance on the look of death" (J. 258). This study has led to the conclusion that Emily Dickinson has rightly been acclaimed as a popular poet ever since the first publication of her poems (1890). This is accountable to the recurring use of two techniques in her poetry. One is the conceptual use of language which lends to her poems an epigrammatic wit and precision ; the other is the conscious use of the riddle as a poetic form to express herself obscurely. Her riddle-like poems are very cryptic and brisk. This conceptual and epigrammatic use of the language, too, contributes to the mythical and oracular touch in her poetry.

So many times, we hear Emily Dickinson speaking strange things or expressing abstract ideas in her typical ecstatic mood, like—"Power is only Pain—Stranded, thro' Discipline" (J. 252) ; "Remorse—is Memory—awake" (J. 744) ; "Doom is the House without the Door"—(J. 475) : "Experience is the Angled Road" (J. 910)—to have a few random examples which can be multiplied to any number. As about the other technique, her poems can form some of the finest riddles ever conceived by human mind. They have wit, irony, comical element, and ambiguity, all the requirements of a successful riddle. Her riddles are literary riddles where description of the object is more important than an answer to it, as in poems—"It sifts from Leaden Sieves"—(J. 311) ; "I like to see it lap the Miles"—(J. 585) ; "I'll tell you how the Sun rose—" (J. 318) ; 'T was like a Maelstrom, with a notch" (V. 414); "A narrow Fellow in the grass" (J. 986), to have a few immediately picked up examples.

In her religious poetry, the use of this technique lends a mystical touch to Emily Dickinson's poetry. The poet is sometimes transported to another world and taken over by "awe". When her consciousness returns to this world, she narrates her experience of the world visited in the form of a riddle. The following poem is a perfect specimen of this technique :

What Inn is this
Where for the night
Peculiar traveller comes ?
Who is the Landlord ?
Where the maids ?
Behold, what curious rooms !
No ruddy fires on the hearth—
No brimming Tankards flow—
Necromancer ! Landlord !
Who are these below ? (J. 115).

It can give an interesting intellectual exercise to the reader to find an answer, which is "Grave !"

As for Emily Dickinson's craftsmanship, numerous explanations can be given to account for her use of capitals, dashes, peculiarities of her syntax, and for obscurity and obliqueness in her poetry. Agreeing with John Crow Ransom, I would comment that they are her "mythopoetic devices." What gives Emily Dickinson's poetry a singular vitality and balance is her harmony between abstraction and sensation. This delicate poise, as Allen Tate has remarked, constitutes the metaphysical quality of her poetry. In this respect, she is more controlled and articulated a poet than either Whitman who plunges into sensations, or Emerson who is too abstract.

Her lyric poetry is a typical spectrum of pictures, colours, and sounds. Even when she writes in a reflective mood, or philosophisizes around certain ideas, the metaphors and images used are those of colors and sound, and the ideas are mostly presented in the form of pictures. Kinaesthetic images are equally prevalent in her poems. Emily Dickinson can be rightly called a poet of "precision," as she can convey more by small phrase units like "Molten Blue," "Alabaster Chambers," "Rafter of Satin," "Cathedral Tunes," "Thunder's Tongue," "Steeples swam in Amethyst," Odor of Colours," "Cherubic Creatures," "Blue Peninsula," and "Route of

Evanescence," than by making imposing philosophical statements about these ideas.

The narrative (word-order) and meaning (word-pattern) in her lyrics attain their technical perfection through vivid and well chosen images of sight, sound, and movement. Thus, along with the metrical rhythm (mostly hymn metre), semantic rhythm (the discursive meaning of the poem), the rhythm of decorum (verbal representation of some highly intense emotional situation), Emily Dickinson is equally adept and perfect in her use of the rhythm of association which is mostly oracular, meditative, irregular, unpredictable, and essentially discontinuous, depending for its technical conciseness and effectiveness on the sound-pattern the poem employs. Invariably all the lyrics in which Dickinson nearly reached the technical, artistic, and thematic perfection employ all these techniques essentially, and primarily, and not incidentally.

Apart from the poems chosen for a detailed analysis in the main body of this study, the poems like "These are the days when Birds Come back" (J. 130), "I taste a liquor never brewed" (J. 214), "There is a certain Slant of light" (J. 258), "This World is not Conclusion" (J. 501), "Further in Summer than the Birds" (J. 1068), "Rearrange a "Wife's" affection !" (J. 1213), "As imperceptibly as Grief" (J. 1540), "We like March" (J. 1213), "Because that you are Going" (J. 1260), "I am alive—"I guess (J 470)" I have a Bird in Spring" (J. 5), "The Sun kept stooping—stooping—low!" (J. 152), "Blazing in Gold and quenching in purple" (J. 228), "What mystery pervades a well" (J. 1400), "I bring an unaccustomed wine" (J 132), "There is a morn by men Unseen—" (J. 24), "I would not paint—a picture—I'd rather be the one" (J. 505)--may be a few examples, the last four being the poems depicting a dreamy or mystical state of mind, and serving good examples of the use of associative rhythm (in Frye's sense) by Emily Dickinson.

Often in Dickinson's poetry, the sense of sight has to be more active than the sense of sound. But the poems expressing some deep emotional turmoil, inner terror and a breakdown of the senses, mostly in death poetry, employ a diction musical and capable of conveying the emotion through corresponding sound-patterns. (For details, see the commentary on "I felt a funeral in my Brain").

Lyric poetry has got as deep a bond with the musical as with the pictorial. Dickinson's poetry is characterized by both, though pictorial often comes over the musical which proves that her visual perceptions were very quick and engrossing. It is due to this singular capability of projecting holistic images by single words or word-units, like, "astonished boughs," "sophistries of June", "Communion in the Haze," "Necromancy Sweet," "Amethyst remembrance," "imperial affliction," of Wizard-erudite," "bright Orthography," "Freckled shrine," "Purples of Ages," "White Sustenance," that she can be compared to the imagist poets of the twentieth century. Visual is at the centre of gravity in Dickinson's poetry, sometimes in harmony with the conceptual as in "The Brain has Corridors—surpassing/ Material Place" (J. 670), and sometimes in harmony with the sense of sound, as in "She sights a Bird—she chuckles—/ She flattens—then she crawls," and "Her Jaws stir—twitching—hungry—" (J. 507). Frequently all the three can be seen in one and the same image: "Low as the laughter of the Cricket/ Loud, as the Thunder's Tongue—" (J. 276); "It fills with Alabaster Wool/ The Wrinkles of the Road"—or "It Ruffles Wrists of Posts/ As Ankles of a Queen—" (J. 311).

III

Thus it can be concluded that Emily Dickinson is an experimenter in verse. This is particularly true of her modernist practice of persona adopted by Eliot, Yeats, and Pound. Her meticulous care with the individual words and nuances of tone is in conjunction with the metaphor she chooses. In her poetry all that we hear is an "authentic voice," sharp and penetrating, speedy in transmitting an emotion, and not a mirror of experience, but the experience itself.

Emily Dickinson's lyrics, though fragmentary in the moods and emotions projected, and unpredictable in the poetic techniques employed, have, however, an integrated and homogeneous poetic thought. At the level of imagination all the poems have got a tendency to stick together and form encyclopaedic aggregrates in their "order" and "clarity," which gleam out involuntarily as the shaping principles of her poetry. One poem studied in proper context to another becomes inexhaustibly suggestive and rich in its meaning. Once viewed as an encyclopaedic whole, a distinctive pattern of imagery, with its own archetypal images of "Awe, ""Home," "Centre", and "Circumference," emerges out of her poetry. These are recurring images which actuate the poet's artistic concern with the authenticity of the poetic vision, and form in turn the tonality of her poetry. Then, there are "modulating," "episodic", and "isolated" images, what may be called the "spectroscopic band of imagery" (a notion derived from Northrop Frye), caused and conditioned by the requirements of the genre, the predilections of the poet, and the emotive and metaphorical concerns of the poems. Thus the metaphors of anguish, pain, bereavement, separation, transport, rapture, ecstasy, intoxication, bliss, God, eternity, heaven and hell, on one hand, and the images of chariot, journey, grave, sea, sun; of tne flying objects like bees, birds, butterflies and wind; flowers, insects, the cycle of seasons (summer being especially dear and meaningful to Emily). equinoxes and solstices, purple and amethyst, on the other, have got a great thematic importance in the mythopoeic poetry of Emily Dickinson, where the passing of the poetic mind from one world to another is the main poetic concern, and the world of nature, incarcerated in the poet's consciousness, the locale of the poetic drama. Therefore, all that the literary criticism can be desired and directed to do with Emily Dickinson's poetry is to make a close analysis of the recurrent images and metaphors and attach them to the central theme and form of her poems. By this process alone can be made intelligible to a common the balance and reconcilement of the discordant elements of Dickinson's poetry, its synthetic and magical power which bring out the "divinest Sense" in the "starkest madness" by telling all the Truth, but telling it slant, and thereby bringing the "superb surprise," the "bright dazzle" and the "infirm Delight" of truth gradually in a circuitous way.

Afterword

She could not live upon the Past
The Present did not know her (J. 1505)

Dickinson critique in the past few years (1979 onwards, to be more specific) has achieved a new remarkability and individuality, as never in the past have there been as many studies in as short a time, and also as diverse in nature as the ones I have listed briefly in my additional bibliography. For the sake of convenience and clarity, and also by virtue of their central emphasis, I would like to describe this teeming body of critical outpourings under two heads: *symptomatic* and *permanent*. *Symptomatic* critics who write under the banner of "feminist criticism", relatively a new emergence in the field of critical scholarship, are vociferously concerned with the fact that Emily Dickinson was a "woman-poet", and also with every event, real or imaginary, that took place in her life. Most of the serious books and scholarly articles published in recent years are surprisingly and self-assuringly having 'feminist' view as the guiding factor of their main argument. These studies include Terrence Diggory's *Shakespeare's Sisters*, Sandra M. Gilbert and Susan Gubar's *The Mad woman in the Attic: The Woman Writer and the Nineteenth-century Literary Imagination*, Margaret Homan's *Women Writers and Poetic Identity*, Suzanne Juhasz's numerous dedicated articles and two very provocative and illuminating books, one under her editorship entitled *Feminist Critics Read Emily Dickinson*, and the other *The Undiscovered Continent: Emily Dickinson and the Space of the Mind* (1984) authored by her, Karl Keller's *The only Kangaroo Among the Beauty: Emily Dickinson and America*, Barbara Mossberg's *Emily Dickinson: When a Writer is a Daughter*, Adrienne Rich's *On Lies, Secrets and Silence*, Vivian Pollak's *The Anxiety of Gender: Emily Dickinson as the Laureate of Sexual Despair*, (1984) and Rebecca Patterson's *Emily Dickinson's Imagery*. The biography-oriented-inventive-genius of these feminist critics (mostly women) has not only aspired to have a positive hold on Dickinson scholarship, it avows to bridge the wide cleavage between the "woman" and the "poet", inculcated and perpetuated by the "traditional criticism." With its stultifying and tepid aesthetic assumptions, and mummifying biographical bonds—characterized by critical blankness and broken commitment to poetry, this *symptomatic* criticism has done precious little, despite its sacred commitments,[1] to reconstitute any *revived* or *new understanding* of the poems, which still present "formidable obstacles."[2]

Despite this relatively murkier character of criticism due to excessive concern with the poet's biography and gender in the larger number of studies mentioned above, there are studies, robustly original and scholarly expiating which I term as *permanent*—like David Porter's *Emily Dickinson's Poetry : The Modern Idiom,* Sharon Cameron's *Lyric Time : Dickinson and the Limits of Genre,* and Joanne Feit Diehl's *Dickinson and the Romantic Imagination.* These three books, each in its own way, attempt to establish *poetic universals* in Emily Dickinson's poetry : Diehl (who is claimed by feminists as their own) by evaluating Dickinson's canterminations with and departures from the Anglo-American Romantic traditions in poetry ; Cameron by making a generic study of Dickinson's poems against the vast tradition of lyric poetry in one direction, and the "oblique dialectic of time and Immortality" in which there lyrics are caught, in another ; and David Porter

[1]I quote here from Suzanne Juhasz's *Feminist Critics Read Emily Dickinson* (Bloomington: Indiana University Press, 1983): "The contribution of feminist criticism to Dickinson studies is twofold. Its first function is revisionary. Traditional criticism has presented Dickinson not only partially but falsely. By splitting her identity into two mutually exclusive elements, "woman" and "poet", traditional criticism has represented two persons, not one." And, "Next, feminist criticism moves from re-interpretation to new kind of interpretation." "Introduction", pp. 1-2.

[2]Joseph Duchac in his immensely useful and informative book *The Poems of Emily Dickinson: An Annotated Guide* (Boston: *G.K. Hall and Co., 1981*) states the position clearly: The process of evaluating and interpreting the poems is clearly in its infancy. More than one fourth of the 1,775 poems and fragments have escaped critical attention entirely." "Introduction" P. VII.

in his majestic book of 1981, an extension to his earlier study of 1966, examines Emily Dickinson as the first *modern* American poet. Porter's objective in writing a new book is noble, laudable, and even enviable,—to break free "the truth of her life" of the "banalities that cling to her reputation," by exhuming her "startling identity."

To these studies may be added a few more titles which, though less affeering in tone, are inviolable in the authenticity of their arguments and unassuming about the critical problems of lasting value they raise. These studies are Ben Kimpel's *Emily Dickinson as Philosopher*, Ann Lilliedahl's *Emily Dickinson in Europe : Her Literary Reputation in Selected Countries*, Wendy Martin's *An American Triptych : Ann Bradstreet, Emily Dickinson, Adrienne Rich* and R.W. Franklin's *The Manuscript Books of Emily Dickinson.*

II

The feminist studies are so well-knit, and so much bound together by a few common bonds, that they are taking care of each other by giving affable ovation to the astute practitioners, in group as well as individually, in their increasingly *heritable* writings. And hence, instead of talking about each feminist critic separately, I will only put across my general remarks about the very substratum of this branch of literary criticism, within the framework of Emily Dickinson's poetry, of course.

Besides, I prefer to talk at some length about the voluminous Franklin book, the publication of which is a significant landmark in Dickinson publication history. Though I have no intention to remain canticent about the importance of Porter's, Cameron's and Diehl's books, I have pretermitted them from a detailed discussions because of their obvious and well-deserved popularity and acceptance in the scholarly circles. I take up here two books for a lengthy discussion—Ben Kimpel's and Ann Lilliedahl's. My arguments in favor of this choice are very natural for reasons unknown, to my mind at least, these books, in spite of their sanguine, scholarly, and research-oriented presentation of mammoth critical problems concerning Emily Dickinson's poetry, in

America as well as in the Continent, have suffered an unwarranted abandon by the seemingly serious Dickinson scholarship. Depending on the mien of a particular critical approach, their arguments may be welcomed or reprobated, as is true of any critical credo. What Ben Kimpel and Ann Lilliedahl have to say interests me, and I have little doubt that it will interest other critics too, for whom Emily Dickinson is still a *crux criticorum.*

My aim here is not to indulge in the languid exercise (as Irving Babbitt would call it) of writing criticism of the criticism, but to bring into a sharper focus, for my own edification and delight as well as the readers', the main trends, directions, and developments that mark the post-modern critical writings on Emily Dickinson.

III

"A concern with gender is central to feminist criticism, which characterizes Dickinson's move into the mind as strategy rather than retreat. Feminist criticism begins with the assumption that gender informs the nature of art, the nature of biography, and the relation between them. Dickinson is a woman poet, and this fact is seen as integral to her identity."[3] Writing about other feminist critics too, Juhasz is confident and patronizing; "In particular, there is a radical difference of perspective, and opinion,...between feminist and traditional critics that is based in their understanding of gender."[4]

And,

"when feminist criticism does turn to Dickinson, its first act is to observe and declare the necessary conjunction between woman and poet."[5] Or, "From feminist perspective, Dickinson's life was neither a flight, nor a cop-out, nor a sacrifice, nor a substitution, but a strategy, a creation, for

---

[3]Suzanne Juhasz, *The Undiscovered Continent: Emily Dickinson and the Space of the mind* (Bloomington: Indiana University Press, 1984), p. 4.

[4]*Ibid*, p. 2.

[5]Suzanne Juhasz, *Feminist Critics Read Emily Dickinson* (Bloomington: Indiana University Press, 1983), p. 9.

enabling her to become the person she was."[6] Thus it is clear that the central concern of the feminist critics is with the gender of the artist, and with the relationship between biography and art. While reading any book or essay by feminist critics, one would frequently come across statements like, "Poetry is always a product of a person,"[7] and "Attention to the relationship between biography and art is a requisite of feminist criticism."[8] As a result of a careful eavesdropping with the inner voice of these critics, two things become quite clear : first—life, gender, and biography have become for them repetitive obsessions, rather than critical revelations. Secondly, they are excessively conscious of their *uniqueness*, the *otherness*, the ways in which they prevaricate from the non-feminist critics, and they decry them as "traditionalists".

I have no qualms about feminist criticism's sensitivity to the components of the female experience in general, but to the assumptions like "Dickinson is a woman poet, and this fact is integral to her identity," or that "Dickinson's identity as a woman generates essential insights about her," I must say that the self-avowed authenticity of these arguments runs the risk of subterfuging its own purpose. If Emily Dickinson is what she is just because she was a woman, the masculine Blakean vigor of her verses will be accounted to what? Closing Dickinson within these confines will mean not finding adequate meaning in her verses. (Even Suzanne Juhasz is quite conscious of many "masculine" qualities of Dickinson's "mind" and "poetry".) The "womanhood" of the poet is just an accident, and should not be used to exemplify so many presuppositions of the feminist critics. Her womanhood can, of course, be used to show the artistic uniqueness of the verses of which the locale was scattered in so many compartments, the womanhood being one of them. That is why, as a poet, Dickinson never felt insecure—she knew it was her lot to live with posterity—*as a poet a priori*—as a woman incidentally. The interaction between literal life-events and poetic reviva-

[6]*Ibid*, p. 10.

[7]*Ibid*, p. 5.

[8]*Ibid*, p. 6.

lism offers strong evidence of Dickinson's artistry. To understand Emily Dickinson fully, we must see her as a New England "woman," wedded to the ideals of American Sublime, but wilfully and obtusely indulged in inverting the traditional Puritan hermeneutics to cater to the demands of her newly formed mythopoeic consciousness. That Emily Dickinson's poetry very often has a female persona behind it, is not accidental, but conscious—and she is never apologetic about it. In a poem liks "Because I could not stop for Death—" she will have her chariot-ride as a woman, and will even inform the imagery of the poem out of a vivid description of her dress, but it is not for literary criticism to pin her down there. At this point I would like to introduce a few lines from a poem of William Blake, to provide a more supple illustration of the relationship between gender and art :

> Bring me my Bow of burning gold :
> Bring me my Arrows of desire :
> Bring me my spear : O clouds unfold !
> Bring me my chariot of fire !

Here in Blake's poem *Milton*, the emphasis is on *me* and *my*; and the poet is riding a chariot that is being drawn by Four Zoas, and is also constituted of them. No reader of this poem will possibly mistake the identity of the poet in terms of the gender. Here the poet *is* a *man* unmistakably. The gender of the poet *has* informed the art—the poem—its similes and metaphors, images and conceits. But should one read, discuss, analyze or criticize this poem for that reason? The twin-poems mentioned above, both having their respective poets riding a chariot as the central image, both overflowing with bacchanal vigor, beauty, charm, and aplomb, both having no ambiguity as far as the identity of the persons who created them is concerned in terms of the gender, do not permit any feminist perspective, or biographical interpretation, to yield their full meaning, unless, ofcourse, these essentially powerful verses have to be converted into something else—for the baneful delight of minor critical documentation.

Moreover, in the case of a poet like Emily Dickinson, the cultural, social, and femilial accretions contradict, repeal and upturn the whole argument of the feminist critics. In her poetry, the New England strains Puritan moorings, Bible, hymn metre, and the fact that, unlike her contemporaries, she carries no explicit influence of the European or British culture, are equally important. Dickinson had to find a rhetoric large enough to accommodate the mood of the Puritan background which her life somewhat respected, but poetry determinedly contorted. We must see her simultaneously as a woman, as a deeply religious but incriminatingly nonconforming Puritan, and as a conscious practitioner of poetry. She blends all these and gives birth to a new vision of art and poetry.

To sum up my comments on feminist critical manifesto : In Emily Dickinson's call the difference has to be made between the fact that she was a woman, and the direct discernible relationship between her poetry and biography. Polly Longsworth in her very recently published book *Austin and Mable* has for the first time revealed a few facts about the first publication of Emily Dickinson's poems and letters with almost a breathtaking accuracy of description and ceremonious fidelity to the fact. Now for once we know what precisely was behind Mable taking such a serious and passionate interest in editing poems for *First Series*, and *Second Series*, and after the latter appeared on November 9, 1981, why she showed so much eagerness to publish Dickinson's letters, which she could, ultimately, under the firm and rigid vigilance of Austin, after a hard work of three years. During the period when Mabel was enthusiastically and sensitively working on the project of collecting and transcribing Emily Dickinson's letters for their eventual publication, "Austin and Vinnie gradually told her," as Longsworth has put it, "many things about the Dickinson upbringing in the Homestead that illuminated the contents and aided in establishing the dates of some poems."[9] A piece of information that is especially revealing in the context of feminist critics' grudge against traditional critics for splitting Emily Dickinson's personality into two—a *woman* and an

[9]Polly Longsworth, *Austin and Mabel*, (New York: Farrar. Straus, 1984), p. 373.

artist, is this : "The project demanded enormous tact and patience, but gradually Mabel accumulated hundreds of letters, enough for a pair of volumes. *Some like those to the Norcross cousins, were gentle and intimate* ; *in others,* *Emily "posed",* as Austin termed it, *displaying artist's quizzical stance toward life around her.*"[10] The point that I am trying to stress may be worded like this : as a woman, Dickinson is intimate and gentle in human relations—as an artist, she is tough and inflexible.

I should once again like to repeat that in Emily Dickinson's case, the meaning of a poem arises from its relation to other poems written on the same theme ; from the gulf of time between the initial creation of a poem, and the poet's inevitable revisit to it—to supply the variants ; from infinite elusive contexts of her life and reading spread throughout her poetry ; from immediate meaning and contextual meanings ; and from the fact that all these contexts are indissoluble and one. The immediate event of her life had to acquire a much larger artistic dimension before it could become ambient in the prisms of poetic emotion expressed through the words. (This point is very well illustrated in last three essays of *Feminist Critics Read Emily Dickinson.*) As is amply recorded to show, life taught Emily fear, bafflement, ambivalence, and despair. But before these all-pervading emotions of life could become an allegorical force in poetry, the life history had to become a rhythm, an idea, a symbol, an image, a metaphor an attuition. Biography, before it could "lapse away" in poetry, as imperceptibly as "Grief" or "Summer", or, in other words, before it could set the tone and direction of her poetry, life history had to be extermalized in the actual poetic combat. When, like nature, Emily Dickinson was "spending with herself" her "Sequestered" life, even her womanhood had to become a wave in the reverberating melody of the poetic consciousness, which had a wider music in its range. Dickinson might have chosen a metaphor for private or extraneous reasons, but, a perfect aesthete as she was, her prime justification for being a poet was her endeavor to master her

[10]*Ibid.* p. 373. (emphasis mine)

art perfectly, to internalise fully in poetic form the commonplace emotion of an ordinary life, to struggle with disharmonies and tensions till they subdue themselves into harmonies and coherences. Each poem is a tiny emblematic story of this struggle, told in a mythic language stunned with mythopoeic imagination, and never the tale of a finally reached triumph (perhaps that is how she never occluded giving variants). Poetry is, in fact, created by a new and fresh interaction, and not a collision, between the tensions of life and the invigorating passion for creativity. This catenates Emily Dickinson with other great poets—Blake's Miltonic preoccupation, Shelley's Promethean revisionism, Keats' consternation at the transitoriness of beauty and art, Eliot's obsession with music in poetry, Wallace Stevens' writhing faith in "supreme fiction"—all are esoteric transumptions of Dickinsonian oppressive obsession with the subtly covert drama of centre and circumference.

Wendy Martin's *The American Triptych* is an effort to draw the outline of the evolution "female poetic" and the "female culture" in Americans, from Puritanism to the present, and also to show how the "American experience has been transformed and transfigured" in the works of the women writers. A new addition to the feminist literary scholarship, the book raises some fundamental questions for the first time, and, with the help of a close discussion of three women poets —Anne Bradstreet, Emily Dickinson, and Adrienne Rich, tries to establish how, while deeply rooted in early American thought, these women poets have created a "counter tradition" of "female aestheticism" in American literature and in the androcentric American society : Ann Bradstreet through severe demands of Puritanism, Emily Dickinson through inspiring and restrictively personalized Romanticism, and Adrienne Rich through private and public feminism. In American "female poetic" the "nature is not subordinate to reason," and "genius, literary or otherwise, is not perceived as male energy uncontaminated by female power."[11] The

[11]Wendy Martin, *An American Triptych: Ann Bradstreet, Emily Dickinson, Adrienne Rich*, (Chapel Hill: The University of North Carolina Press, 1984), p. 10.

uniqueness of this book lies in its attempt to relate the work of these poets to the main tradition of American experience. Emily in this process has been brought close to her contemporaries and male counterparts—Howthorne, Meluille, and Thoreau—in her fervent rejection of values of the rapidly industrializing North-eastern societies. After Roy Harvey Pearce's *The Continuity of American Poetry* published in 1961, where for the first time Emily Dickinson was solidly established as obscure but tremendously powerful poet of the American Renaissance, Martin is the only literary critic who carries on this point for a further discussion.

Emily Dickinson's love affairs obsess Wendy Martin as much as they do other biographical critics. Unlike William H. Shurr whose vote is for Wadsworth, and Dorothy Waugh who gives enough documentary, historical, and circumstantial evidences in favor of Richard Saltar Storrs Dickinson, Martin is more in line with the tradition critics. For her Emily's youthful attachment was with Samuel Bowles, and in maturity "ultimately received Otis Lord's rapturous attention."[12] Wendy's book is remarkable for its pioneering adaptation of the principle of the "female poetic" and its relationship with the main current of American thought, i.e., Puritanisms. Though the banner is again "feminist," the perspective is surprisingly new and adorable.

IV

The publication of *The Manuscript Books of Emily Dickinson* in two volumes under the very responsible and experienced editorship of R.M. Franklin is bound to give a new direction to future Dickinson criticism. For the first time we see the poet at work in trying to bring some system in the otherwise "plated wares" of her creativity. And hence, the judgments now in certain categories of studies have to be informed by the manuscript conventions themselves. Fascicles, as Franklin has put it, can be treated as "artistic gatherings" of the poet. One may infer (with how much certainty, no one knows) that Emily had certain themes and emotional attitudes in the mind

[12] *Ibid.* P. 115.

when she collected her poems into small, self-styled volumes, and literary criticism may seek through them the inner pattern and system of the poet's imagination. For the first time now we have some authentic inside information. This is important since we have least such knowledge about Emily Dickinson who never established any verbal conversational relationship with the world outside.

But many facts are still obscure, the most important of them being the time of the composition of a poem, and also, 'what' and 'how' did poet feel about the best of her work. And, why did she start this form of book-making, and why did she end it abruptly during 1870s? Though Franklin tries to give some probable explanation as to why Emily once again returned to the loose sheet method,[13] it remains a conjecture in the absence of any definite evidence. And also, what were the guiding factors in Emily deciding to include or join in a particular fascicle a particular poem? Why did she not give any titles, headings, or dates to the fascicles, which she prepared so operosely, preferably in the same sort of ink or handwriting, and on a similar sheet of paper?

Once these subjective omissions and doubts about the fascicles are cleared, the earnest Dickinson researchers may use the Manuscript Books "as gatherings interrelated by theme, imagery, emotional movement." Now Emily Dickinson's poetic process can be subjected to a closer scrutiny and analysis, and a method may emerge, though many details, as pointed out, will still remain elusive.

As a result of close look at Dickinson fascicles, very few rationally drawn conclusions emerge :

1. The bound units and unbound sheets combined, the larger portion of the poems (about two-third or more)

---

[13]"One motive that Emily Dickinson had in constructing these books was to reduce disorder in her manuscripts." And "The growing number of the fascicles must have made tangible to Emily Dickinson her poetic achievement, but as they multiplied, the simple order they provided must have become an increasingly difficult virtue." (PX) R.W. Franklin *The Manuscript Books of Emily Dickinson* (Cambridge: The Harvard University Press, 1981) pp. IX and X.

has been used by the poet in her own "handwriting" and "handwinging" for the "bookmaking."

2. The poems included in the fascicles are surely among Dickinson's "Elect," no matter when they were written, and how many years elapsed between their composition and transcription. The interesting thing to note here is that this is the only form of publication, as unique as the verses themselves, and as private and selective as the "Divine majority" of her artistic moorings, that the poet allowed for herself.
3. The initial enthusiasm of Lavinia, and the hard work put in by Mabel Loomis Todd on the "scraps" of Emily Dickinson, before the *First Series* (1890) could come out, was decidedly inspired by these Manuscript Books.
4. The critics may feel now more consciously concerned with Dickinson's unusual punctuation and capitalization.
5. The alternate readings were not given immediately after a poem was composed, but came later as the poet "revisited" her *mental offsprings* after several years for her own rejoicing, or to send them to some friend in a letter.
6. It is proved now beyond doubt that Emily Dickinson's reverence for her creativity remained absolutely inflexible throughout her life.
7. Due to this archaic artistic expressionism of the poet in some visible form, multiple confusions could be avoided, as is clear if one compares these *orderly volumes* with the worksheets of the later years when Emily was no more interested in bringing any external order into her creations.
8. Even while reading fascicles, a critic has to remain petulantly conscious of the fact that the dates given there are not invariably the dates of the *composition* of the poems ; they merely indicate the speculative dates of the *transcriptions*, which survive in divided hands now. In certain cases, the date when the individual *poem* was sent to a friend is well known,

and that merely tells a time by which the poem *did* exist—for how long, no one knows. In such cases, only the penmanship can give little but tenable help.

9. As pointed out, Emily Dickinson gave variant readings while making copies for the friends, and this proves that every time she read her manuscripts, she *re-collected* the artistic-creative energy, which obviously was not a spent force once the poem was complete. And this further proves that life stoplessly provided her with enough to take and improve her poems further. By this process, Emily Dickinson joins the creative cult of great many artists, on the path of a broadened tradition of poetry on one hand, and unbroken individual uniqueness on the other. We have the notebooks and worksheet drafts of Beethoven, Henry Adams, Shakespeare, Milton, and T.S. Eliot. This process was a joy, an ecstasy, for Emily Dickinson; it has made posterity's job tough and challenging. But the demand of the critical craftsmanship is to grapple with the challenge, and not seek a "light escape" in biographical obscurantism.

If T.H. Johnson's variorum edition was one epoch-making event in the flurries of Dickinson publication history, probably the most complicated and highly baffling that ever existed, Franklin's facsimile reproduction of Dickinson fascicles is another; and from the point of view of literary criticism, perhaps, even greater.

Based on Emily Dickinson's fascicles, William H. Shurr's *The Marriage of Emily Dickinson* (*1983*) is a serious and sensible study, though an effort to reify many a puzzling barrier of Dickinson biography has straggled his arguments to a certain extent. In the very beginning of the book, while acknowledging his debt to the published criticism on Emily Dickinson, Shurr declares: "It will be recognized immediately that behind this book stands the editorial work of Ralph W. Franklin. Since the death of Emily Dickinson no one has been able to study her poems exactly as Dickinson left them, until the reconstruction of the original booklets was published by Franklin."[14] Against this background, William Shurr's statements in the next few pages of the book astonished me totally. According to Shurr, R.W. Franklin has *warned* us "against the attempt to read the fascicles as "careful constructs governed by theme. imagery, narrative and dramatic movement, or similar pursuit." Franklin argued that Dickinson's fascicles were merely gatherings of her best poems—indeed that they are nearly the only poems of hers we have from the years she was constructing the fascicles."[15] Though I have earlier mentioned briefly what Franklin has to say about fascicles in his latest book in two volumes in 1981 from Harvard, I quote Franklin once again in full for the ready reference of the reader: "A facsimile edition is of particular importance to Dickinson studies, for the manuscripts of this poet resist translation into the conventions of print. Formal features like her unusual punctuation and capitalization, line and stanza divisions, and display of alternate readings are a source of continuing critical concern. Because she saw no poem through the press and left her manuscripts unprepared for print, judgments must be informed by the manuscript conventions themselves. Perhaps no less important, interest has developed in the fascicles as artistic gatherings—as gatherings intrarelated by theme, imagery, emotional movement. In general, we need to understand why she assembled the fascicles—by what principles and for what purposes—and to have them available in the way she viewed them."[16] In the light of the above, Shurr's presentation of Franklin's arguments appears misleading and *careless*. To Shurr's presumption that "Each fascicle has a core of poems directly related to Dickinson's love affair, and, later, to her anomalous marriage,"[17] and, to his extensive researches on determining the identity of Emily's beloved, the conclusions drawn by Dorothy Waugh, as a result of long years of research and careful study of the "letters, journals,

[14]William H. Shurr, *The Marriage of Emily Dickinson* (Kentucky: the University Press of Kentucky, 1983) from Acknowledgments.

[15]*Ibid.* p. 3.

[16]Franklin, "Introduction", p. IX.

[17]Shurr, p. 7.

wills, deeds, town-meeting records, court records, and town, country, and state histories"[18]—are authentic in contents and convincing in logic: "We will never know conclusively who the man was who awakened the turmoil in Emily Dickinson's heart that sent many of the finest love poems in any language to paper; but there are extensive grounds to intelligent, deeply thoughful speculation founded on thorough research and familiarity with the period and place."[19] While Shurr's "intelligent deeply thoughtful speculation" is in favor of Reverend Charles Wadsworth, a priest from Philadelphia, Dorothy Waugh's is in favor of another presbyterian priest—Richard Salter Storrs Dickinson. Here I may, perhaps, add that at the present state of knowledge in this particular matter, it is difficult to find somebody who is more acquainted with "the poet's period, place, and the people who surrounded her," than Dorothy Waugh.

V

Since Emily Dickinson wrote at a time when American literature was considered matured enough to be worthy of comparison with the finest in European literature, and also because her themes of nature, death, love, religion, and immortality are as universal as the treatment Puritan and New Englandly, she was taken seriously in Europe even before the publication of the Harvard edition of her poems. (That is why not only Emily Dickinson, but almost all the major American writers have been treated with a serious critical concern in Europe much before the turn of the century, and there have been exclusive studies on authors like Edgar Allen Poe, Henry James, Ernest Hemingway, Herman Melville and Nathaniel Hawthorne. And well-established American critics, in turn, have taken a serious note of these studies).

In *Emily Dickinson's Reputation in Europe* by Ann Lilliedahl, for the first time a reader *in English* is presented with

[18]Dorothy Waugh, *Emily Dickinson's Beloved, A Surmise*, (New York: Vantage Press, 1975) from the Foreword.

[19]*Ibid.* p. 1.

critical scholarship on Emily Dickinson produced outside the United States, and in languages other than English. The European countries covered are the following: Sweden, Norway, Denmark, France, Germany, German and French-speaking Switzerland, and former Danish colony of Iceland. The book is a candid and honest representation of the critical pronouncements, and not a criticism of criticisms. The chapter division is based on countries and culture groupings; and, as the time covered is generously long—since Emily Dickinson's death in 1886 to 1977—, a strict chronology has been observed. The chief merit of this book lies in its accuracy with regard to chronology and translations, and otherwise, in simplicity, directness, and straightforwardness of the style.

At the end of the book, there is a coordinated evaluation of the entire European criticism on Emily Dickinson, with an attempt to relate different studies to one another. During this process of coordination, extra-critical-reference-points, like national literary tastes, cultural moorings, social, political, and historical factors etc., have been brought into sharp focus. One interesting conclusion drawn by the author is that European criticism ofEmily Dickinson is the "cultural-psychological-response" of the countries concerned. For example, in small countries like Sweden and Finland, the theory of "the art of loneliness" is appropriately responsible for giving Emily Dickinson's poetry that warm reception, full of understanding, which a poeple with the experience of "both physical and spiritual isolation" alone can accord.[20]

Similarly in France, the "passion for exploring anything truly challenging apparently found outlet in the unconventional poetic expression of Emily Dickinson."[21] Moreover, "not only in literature but in other art forms as well, women had been recognized for centuries," and this made the French atmosphere especially suitable for Dickinson's acceptance.[22]

---

[20]Ann Lilliedahl, *Emily Dickinson in Europe: Her Literary Reputation in Selected Couctries*, (*Washington*: University Press of America, *1981*) P. 167,

[21]*Ibid*, P. 171.

[22]*Ibid*, P. 171.

Secondly, whereas traditional critics of Emily Dickinson have been more concerned with the thwarting presence of the themes of love, death, nature, immortality etc., the focus of the European critics has been on soul's selection of her own society, on the celebration of the individual: " The "celebration of the individual" is regarded as a significant overall theme in all of the nations surveyed."[23] Thirdly, as a sequel to the above two, more attention has been paid to the uniqueness and individuality of Dickinson's style. The way Emily Dickinson used her language impressed European critics most.

As one views these pieces of criticism more and more objectively, the impression that mounts up is simple—whereas the consuming concern of the modern American critics is to judge the 'loner artist' like Emily Dickinson by the traditional reference points of theme and biography, and to prove that the artist is a parasite to the events of life and to the interactions with people and surroundings, the "European critics in general—where a more traditionally oriented outlook might have been expected—have tended to value Dickinson as the artist in opposition to a traditional background, a conventional society, and the conventions of her mother tongue—an existential success."[24]

VI

Kimpel's *Emily Dickinson as Philosopher* addresses itself to a strong current invisibly flowing all through Dickinson poems. It is an ideal presentment of a permanent feature of Emily Dickinson's poetry. I deal with the *process* of the poet's experience, Kimpel with the *precept* of it. A premise made by T.H. Johnson three decades ago that "philosophic problems" are central in majority of the poems written by Emily Dickinson meets a full length treatment for the first time in this book. The thoughts of the well known philosophers on some of the problems concerning reflective ideas on poetry, life, love, nature, religion, death, and immortality

[23]*Ibid*, P. 174.

[24]Ben Kimpel, P. 181.

are placed side by side Emily Dickinson's poetic utterances—and in this way, at times, the slanted meaning of some of the poems can be understood more decisively.

Kimpel's book focuses attention mainly on one important aspect of Emily Dickinson's writings, and that is, "*her reflecting* which would ordinarily be *regarded as a philosophy* about human life in its relations to other human beings, to nature, and to a reality other than nature and human life, which latter consideration could be regarded as an expression of the religious aspect of her life."[25]

As for example—while discussing Emily Dickinson's treatment of love, Kimpel brings about a very appropriate and striking comparison—a reference to Plato's Symposium, where, at a banquet, a number of intellectuals, philosophers, and writers express their views on *love*. Among those present were : the writers Agathon; the author of *Clouds*, Aristophanes; the aristocrat Alcibiades ; Plato's disciple Phaedrus; a medical-guide-member Eryximachus; and Socrates. Each one airs his ideas on love. Socrates is the last one to state what he thinks of love, which, 'Socrates confesses, he has learned from the priestress Diotima. And "what is significant in Plato's dialogue is that her interpretation of love is expressed in the language of religion, just as are many of Emily Dickinson's. Diotima interprets love both as mortal and also as immortal, and so both as human and also as divine. It is this same ambivalent nature which is characteristic of Emily Dickinson's references to love. She declares : "Love is Immortality,/Nay, it is Deity."[26] Kimpel even concludes that Emily Dickinson might well have taken this idea from Pre-Christian Greek Philosophy, rather than from Christianity.

Similarly, the Poem "This world is not Conclusion" (J. 501) is quoted and discussed by Kimpel as "a phenomenological analysis of the type of struggle through which some religious individuals go in their attempt to clarify for themselves the beliefs which they can subscribe as true. This poem in every respect is, therefore, a parallel of St. Augustine's *Confessions*,

[25]Ben Kimpel, *Emily Dickinson as Philosopher*, (New York: Edwin Mellon Press, 1981), *Preface*, X.

[26]Kimpel, pp. 249-50.

in which he acknowledges the temptestuous upheaval in his life to think through the conflicting reasons for not believing as a Christian and also for believing as a Christian. Basic to this poem is a confident affirmation that there is an order of reality which is other than the world, and is transcendent of it in the sense that it is "beyond" it."[27]

The story of Emily Dickinson's *unnamed*, undeclared, unpublished, and unrevealed poems, in Kimpel's opinion, is much the same as that of Spinoza's *Ethics*. Of the total body of her poetry, Emily Dickinson left at least two-thirds in small 'books' of her own type—the fascicles (grouped and filled up by the poet between 1858 and 1872). Similarly, Spinoza's *Ethics* remained unpublished during his life time. And then, after his death, the book, one most remarkably outstanding in the history of philosophy, was found along with his letters and other unpublished works; and so, to quote Kimpel, "one may say of her poetry what Professor Fuller has said of Spinoza's *Ethics*: "*after his death, it was found in his room along with his letters and other unpublished work—These comprised his entire estate—one of the richest ever left by any man.*"[28] The power and tenuosity of Emily Dickinson's language receive a special attention in this book too. But the tone of the book some times becomes too much loaded with philosophic opinions, and the conclusions—solitary contemplations of the author.

In this eddy of directions, what is the achievement of Dickinson critical scholarship ? For one thing, radical, unorthodox implication of Dickinson's verses has been saved for future, thanks to the efforts of a whole generation of critics. But, by inevitably adopting a "feminist" and biographical" view, the criticism has become biased. Their methods remain strong, but the insights—fragile and fumbling. Of course, to stand directly against this approach may create another king of bias. My frank commitment throughout the pages of this book has been toward the artistic provisions that the exiguous and arcane verses of Emily Dickinson

---

[27] *Ibid*, p. 228.

[28] Kimpel p. 19.

disseminate. The predeterministic whims of the biographical critics which these years endured have adumbrated and disturbed more than ever an understanding and appreciation of the *poems* which, having seen as if an aeon after their composition, deplorably hold *alone* the keys to their chanted profundities and agonizing ambiguities.

A modern American poet Galway Kinnell, while writing about another poet, Francois Villon, remarks : "Perhaps a certain contempt for poetry is behind a preoccupation with a poet's life."[29] Thinking of Emily Dickinson, who can risk identifying "the beloved" in a consciously obliterated and hermetically sealed life?

And I conclude now by taking note of Helen Vendler's latest review-article entitled "The Road Taken," writing which, as one clearly sees, Vendler was not having Emily Dickinson even remotely in her vision, but could not help expressing the grief and shock of a sharp and sensitive critical mind at the stubbornness of biographical inquisitiveness. Not surprisingly, the poet who, without the critic's knowledge, made her invisible appearance as the uncontested prototype of this stubborn scrutiny was no other than Emily Dickinson, joined by Keats Wallace Stevens, of course : "The context of the life may be positively harmful to the poet's reputation, as we know from such reductive phrases as "The Belle of Amherst" for Emily Dickinson or the "Cockney poet" for Keats;" then Vendler goes further, but comes back to Emily Dickinson once again : "The intuitive conviction that art and life must stand in some relation to each other justifies literary biography; but of course the genre succeeds best when the artist has had a life of marked intellectual and social incident (T.S. Eliot, Robert Lowell) and is least helpful with respect to artists whose lives have been quiet or obscure (Emily Dickinson, Wallace Stevens)."[30]

[29]Quoted by Richard Howard in his book *Alone with America* : (New York: Atheneum, 1980), p. 304.

[30]Helen Vendler, "The Road Taken" in *The New York Times*, october 84, 1984.

Additional Emily Dickinson Bibliography : 1979-84

Baym, Nina. "God, Father, and Lover in Emily Dickinson's Poetry." In *Puritan Influences in America*, ed. Emory Elliott, pp. 193-209. Urbana : University of Illinois Press, 1979.

Burbick, Joan. "'One Unbroken Company' : Religion and Emily Dickinson." *New England Quarterly* 53, no. 1 (March 1980) : 62-75.

Cameron, Sharon. *Lyric Time : Dickinson and the Limits of Genre.* Baltimore : The Johns Hopkins University Press, 1979.

Diehl, Joanne Feit. *Dickinson and the Romantic Imagination.* Princeton : Princeton University Press, 1981.

Diehl, Joanne Feit. "Dickinson and Bloom : An Antithetical Reading of Romanticism." *Texas Studies in Literature and Language* 23, no. 3 (September 1981).

Diggory, Terrence. "Armed Women, Naked Men : Dickinson, Whitman, and Their Successors." In *Shakespeare's Sisters*, ed. Sandra M. Gilbert and Susan Gubar, pp. 135-50. Bloomington : Indiana University Press, 1979.

Duchac, Joseph. *The Poems of Emily Dickinson : an Annotated Guide.* Boston : G.K. Hall and Co., 1979.

Franklin, R. Williams. *The Manuscript Books of Emily Dickinson.* Cambridge : The Belknap Press of Harvard University Press, 1981.

Gelpi, Albert J. "Emily Dickinson and the Deerslayer : The Dilemma of the Woman Poet in America." In *Shakespeare's Sisters*, ed. Sandra M. Gilbert and Susan Gubar, pp. 122-34. Bloomington : Indiana University Press, 1979.

Gilbert, Sandra M., and Susan Gubar. "A Woman White : Emily Dickinson's Yarn of Pearl." In *The Madwoman in the Attic : The Woman Writer and the Nineteenth-Century Literary Imagination.* pp. 581-650. New Haven and London : Yale University Press, 1979.

Homans, Margaret. *Woman Writers and Poetic Identity.* Princeton : Princeton University Press, 1980.

Juhasz, Suzanne. "The 'Undiscovered Continent' : Emily Dickinson and the Space of the Mind." *Missouri Review* 3, no. 1 (Fall 1979) : 86-97.

Juhasz, Suzanne. "'To Make a Prairie' : Language and Form in Emily Dickinson's Poems About Mental Experience." *Ball State University Forum* 21. no. 2 (Spring 1980) 12-25.

Juhasz, Suzanne. "'Peril as a Possession' : Emily Dickinson and Crisis." *Massachusetts Studies in English* 7, no. 4, and 8, no. 1(1981) : 28-39.

Juhasz, Suzanne. "'But Most, Like Chaos' : Emily Dickinson Measures Pain." *The American Transcendental Quarterly* 43(Summer 1981) 225-40.

Juhasz, Suzanne. *Feminist Critics Read Emily Dickinson.* Bloomington : Indiana University Press, 1983.

Juhasz, Suzanne. The Undiscovered Continent : *Emily Dickinson and the Space of the Mind.* 1984.

Keller, Karl. *The Only Kangaroo Among the Beauty* : *Emily Dickinson and America.* Baltimore : Johns Hopkins University Press, 1979.

Kimpel, Ben. *Emily Dickinson as Philosopher.* New York : The Edwin Mellon Press, 1981.

Lilliedahl, Ann. *Emily Dickinson in Europe* : *Her Literary Reputation in Selected Countries.* Washington : University Press of America, 1981.

Longsworth, Polly. *Austin and Model.* New York : Farrar. Straus, Gironx, 1984.

Martin, Wendy. *An American Triptych* : *Ann Bradstreet, Emily Dickinson, Adrienne Rich.* Chapel Hill : The University of North Carolina Press, 1984.

Mossberg, Barbara Antonina Clarke. *Emily Dickinson* : *When a Writer Is a Daughter.* Bloomington : Indiana University Press, 1982.

Patterson, Rebecca. *Emily Dickinson's Imagery. Amherst* : University of Massachusetts Press, 1979.

Pollak, Vivian R. "Thrist and Starvation in Emily Dickinson's Poetry." *American Literature* 51(1979) : 33-49.

Pollak, Vivian R. "Emily Dickinson's Literary Allusions." *Essays in Literature* (Western Illinois University) 1 : 54-68.

Pollak, Vivian R. *The Anxiety of Gender*: *Emily Dickinson as the Laureate of Sexual Despair.* 1984.

Porter, David. *Dickinson* : *The Modern Idiom.* Cambridge : Harvard University Press, 1981.

Rich, Adrienne. "Vesuvius at home : The power of Emily Dickinson." In *On Lies, Secrets* and *Silence,* pp. 157-84. New York : W.W. Norton and Co., Inc., 1979.

Shullenberger, William and Candice Ward, eds. *Massachuesetts Studies in English* : Special Issue on Emily Dickinson. Vol. VIII No. 1. Amherst : University of Massachusetts, 1981.

Shurr ,William H. *The Marriage of Emily Dickinson* : Kentucky : the University Press of Kentucky, 1983.

SELECTED BIBLIOGRAPHY

Abrams, M.H. *The Mirror and the Lamp : Romantic Theory and Critical Tradition.* New York : W. W. Norton and Co., 1958.

...... "Structure and Style in Greater Romantic Lyric." In *From Sensibility to Romanticism.* Ed. Frederick W. Hilles and Harold Bloom. New York: Oxford University Press, 1965. pp. 527-60.

Adams, Richard P. "Pure Poetry: Emily Dickinson." *Tulane Studies in English,* 7 (1957), 133-52.

Allen, Gay W. "Emily Dickinson." In *American Prosody.* New York : American Book Co., 1935, pp. 307-21.

Anderson, Charles R. *Emily Dickinson's Poetry : Stairway of Surprise.* New York: Holt, Rinehart & Winston, 1960.

...... "The Conscious Self in Emily Dickinson's Poetry." *American Literature,* 31 (1959), 290-308.

...... "The Trap of Time in Emily Dickinson's Poetry." *Journal of English Literary History.* 26 (1959), 402-24.

Angott, Charles. "Emily Dickinson and Religious Poetry." *Tomorrow,* VII (Dec., 1947), 24.

Avanzo, Mario L. "Unto the White Creator : the Snow of Dickinson and Emerson." *New England Quarterly,* 45 (1972), 278-80.

Avanzo, Mario L. "Dickinson's 'The Reticent Volcano' and Emerson." *American Transcendental Quarterly,* 14 (1972), 11-13.

Avery, Christine. "Science, Technology, and Emily Dickinson." *Bulletin of the British Association for American Studies.* (Dec., 1964), 47-55.

Barnes, Hazel E. *Humanistic Existentialism . The Literature of Possibility.* Lincoln : University of Nebraska Press, 1959.

Barret, William. *Irrational Man: A Study in Existential Philosophy.* New York: Doubleday and Co., Anchor Books, 1962.

Beaty Jerome and William H. Matchett. *Poetry: From Statement to Meaning.* New York: Oxford University Press, 1965.

Beauvoir. Simone de. *The Ethics of Ambiguity,* Translated by Bernard Frechtmon. New York : Citadel Press, 1967.

Benziger James. *Images of Eternity: Studies in the Poetry of Religious Vision from Wordsworth to T.S. Eliot.* Carbondale: Southern Illinois University Press, 1962.

Berrenson, Andrienne. "Emily Dickinson's Social Studies:A Dissenting View.' *Western Humanities Review,* VI (1952), 351-62.

Bianchi, Martha Dickinson. *The Life and Letters of Emily Dickinson.* London: Jonathan Cape, 1924.

...... *The Complete Poems of Emily Dickinson.* Boston: Little, Brown, & Co., 1930.

Bingham, Millicent Todd. *Ancestors's Brocades : The Literary Debut of Emily Dickinson.* New York : Harper & Bros., 1945.

...... *Emily Dickinson : A Revelation.* New York : Harper & Bros., 1954.

Birdsall, Virginia Ogden. "Emily Dickinson's Intruder in the Soul." *American Literature*, 37 (1965), 54-64.

Blackmur, R.P. "Emily Dickinson : Notes on Prejudice and Fact." In *Language As Gesture.* New York : Harcourt, Brace, and Co., 1952. pp. 25-50.

Blake, Caesar R. and Carlton F. Wells, eds. *The Recognition of Emily Dickinson : Selected Criticism Since 1890.* Ann Arbor : University of Michigan Press, 1964.

Blake, William, *Poetry and Prose.* Ed. David V. Erdman: Commentary by Harold Bloom. New York: Doubleday & Co., 1965.

Bodkin, Maud. *Archetypal Patterns in Poetry : Psychological Studies of Imagination.* London : Oxford University Press, 1963.

Bogan, Louise. *Acknowledgement in American Poetry.* Chicago : Henry Regenery, 1951.

Bradley, Sculley, Richmond C.B,, and E, Hudson Long. *The American Tradition in Literature.* New York : W.W. Norton & Co., Inc., 1961.

Brett, R.L. *Reason and Imagination : A Study of Form and Meaning in Four Poems,* London : Oxford University Press, 1969.

Brooks, Cleanth. *The Well Wrought Urn : Studies in the Structure of Poetry.* New York : Harcourt, Brace, & World, 1947.

...... and Robert Penn Warren. *Understanding Poetry.* New York : Holt, Rinehart and Winston, 1960.

Buckingham, Wills J. *Emily Dickinson : An Annotated Bibliography.* Bloomington : Indiana University Press, 1970.

Calderwood, James L. and Harold E. Toliver, eds. *Perspectives on Poetry.* London : Oxford University Press, 1968.

Cambon, Glauco. "Dickinson : Confrontation of the Self with Otherness in the Inner Space." In *The Inclusive Flame : Studies in American Poetry.* Bloomington : Indiana University Press, 1963 .

...... "Emily Dickinson and the Crises of Self-Reliance." In *Transcendentalism and Its Legacy.* Ed. Myron Simon and Thronton H. Parsons. Ann Arbor : University of Michigan Press, 1966.

Cameron, Kenneth Walter. "Emily Dickinson and Hesperian Depression." *American Transcendental Quarterly*, 14 (1972), 184-5.

Cameron, Sharon. "Naming as History : Dickinson's Poems of Definition." *Critical Inquiry.* 5, II (Winter 1978), 232-51.

Campbell, Joseph. *The Hero with a Thousand Faces.* New York: Pantheon Books, 1961.

...... *The Masks of God : Oriental Mythology.* New York : Viking Press, 1962.

...... *The Masks of God : Creative Mythology.* New York : Viking Press, 1968.

Cappes, Jack Lee. *Emily Dickinson's Reading : 1836-86*. Cambridge, Mass : Harvard University Press, 1966.

Cassirer, Ernst. *Language and Myth*. Translated by Susanne K. Langer. New York : Dover Publications, 1953.

Chaliff, Cynthia, "The psychology of Economics in Emily Dickinson." In *Literature and Psychology*. University of Hartford, 1968.

Chase, Richard. *Walt Whitman Reconsidered*. New York : William Sloane Associates, 1955.

...... *Emily Dickinson. American Men of Letters Series*. New York : William Sloane Associates, 1951.

Choron, Jacques. *Death and Western Thought*. New York : Collier Books, 1963.

Cirlot, J.E. *A Dictionary of Symbols*. Translated by Jack Sage. New York : Philosophical Library, 1962.

Clendenning, Sheila T. *Emily Dickinson : A Bibliography 1850-1966*. Kent, Ohio; Kent State University Press, 1968.

Cody, John. *After Great Pain: The Inner Life of Emily Dickinson*. Cambridge: Harvard University Press, 1971.

Cohen, Hennig. *The American Experience: Approaches to the Study of the United States*. Faridabad : Thompson Press, 1972.

Collins, John Clurton. *Studies in Poetry and Criticism*. London: George Bell & Sons, 1905.

Cunliffe, Marcus. "Minor Key (Emily Dickinson and Others)," In *The Literature of the United States*. Penguin Books: Harmondsworth, 1959.

Curren, George. "Emily Dickinson and Religion." *Smith College Monthly*, II (November, 1941), 7-9.

Curtis, Jared R. "Edward Taylor and Emily Dickinson: Voices and Visions." *Susqueharinia University Studies*, VII (June, 1964), 159-67.

Curti, Merle. *The Growth of American Thought*. New York: Harper & Bros., 1951.

D'Arcy, Martin C. *The Mind and Heart of Love*. New York: World Publishing Co., 1964.

Daiches, David. *Critical Approaches to Literature*. Bombay: Orient Longmans, 1967.

Davidson, Frank. "This Consciousness': Emerson and Dickinson." *Emerson Society Quarterly*, 44 (1966), 2-7.

Davidson, J. "Emily Dickinson and Issac Watts." *Boston Public Library Quarterly*, 6 (1954), 141-49.

Davis, Thomas M., ed. 14 *by Emily Dickinson : With Selected Criticism. Chicago:* Scott, Foresman, & Co., 1964.

Deutch, Babetts. "Poetry at the Mid Century." *Virginia Quarterly Review*, XXVI (1950), 67-75.

...... *Poetry in Our Time: A Critical Survey of Poetry in the English-Speaking World, 1900-1960*. New York: Doubleday, Anchor Books, 1963.

Donogue, Denis. *Emily Dickinson*. Minneapolis; University of Minnesota Press, 1969.

...... "Emily Dickinson'. In *Connoisseur of Chaos: Ideas of Order in Modern American Poetry.* New York: Macmillan, 1965,

Duncon, Douglas. *Emily Dickinson.* Edinburgh, 1965.

Duncan, Douglas. *Emily Dickinson.* Edinburgh and London : Oliver and Boyd, 1965.

Dunne, John S. *The City of Gods: A Study in Myth and Morality.* New York: The Macmillan Company, 1965,

Eliade, Mircea. *The Myth of the Eternal Return.* New York: Pantheon, 1954.

...... *Myth and Reality.* New York: Harper & Row, 1968.

Eliot, T.S. *Collected Poems: 1909-35.* London: Faber & Faber, 1958,

...... *Four Quartets.* London: Faber & Faber, 1959.

Emerson, Ralph Waldo. *Essays.* Introduction by Shiv Kumar. New Delhi: Eurasia Publishing House, 1965.

Empson, William. *Seven Types of Ambiguity,* Penguin Books: Harmondsworth, 1961.

Eulert, Donald. "Emily Dickinson's Certain Slant of Light." *American Transcendental Quarterly,* 14 (1972), 164-6.

Fallico, Arturo B. *The Quest for Authentic Existence.* Stockton, Cal., College of the Pacific Publications in Philosophy, 1958.

...... *Art and Existentialism.* Englewood Cliffs. N. Jersey: Prentice-Hall, 1962.

Fasel, Ida. "Emily Dickinson's Walden." *Iowa English Yearbook,* 7 (1962). 22-28.

Ferlazzo, Paul J. *Emily Dickinson.* Boston, 1976.

Ferm, Vergilius. *A Brief Dictionary of American Superstitions.* New York: Philosophical Library, 1952.

Feidelson Charles Jr. *Symbolism and American Literature.* Chicago: University of Chicago Press, 1953.

...... and Brodtkorb, Paul Jr., eds. *Interpretations of American Literature.* New York: Oxford University Press, 1959.

Fiedler, Leslie A. *Love and Death in the American Novel.* New York: Criterion Books, 1960.

Fisher, C.J. "Emily Dickinson as a Latter-Day Metaphysical Poet." *Atlantic Transcendental Quartely,* 1 (1969), 77-81.

Fiske, Nathan W. *Sermons and Other Writings.* Ed. Haman Humphry. Amherst, Massachusetts: J.S. & Co., 1850.

Fnich, Wallace H. "The Poetry of Emily Dickinson." *Religion in life.* II (1933), 194-202.

Ford, Thomas W. *Heaven Beguiles the Tired: Death in the Poetry of Emily Dickinson.* Alabama: University of Alabama Press, 1966.

Forstman. H. Jackson. *Word and Spirit: Calvin's Doctrine of Biblical Authority.* California: Stanford University Press, 1962.

Franklin, R.W. *The Editing of Emily Dickinson: A Reconsideration.* Madison: University of Wisconsin Press, 1967.

Fraser, G.S. *The Modern Writer and His World*. Penguin Books: Harmondsworth, 1970.

Fraser, Robert S. *The Margaret Jane Collection of Emily Dickinson*. Introduction by Richard M. Ludwig. Presented to the Princeton University Library, June 7. 1969.

Frazer, J.C. *The Golden Bough: A Study in Magic and Religion*. London: Macmillan & Co., 1963.

Frye, Northrop, *Anatomy of Criticism: Four Essays*. Princeton: Princeton University Press, 1957.

...... *Fables of Identity: Studies in Poetic Mythology*. New York: Harcourt, Brace, & World, 1963.

...... *A Study of English Romanticism*. New York; Random House, 1968.

...... ed. *Romanticism Reconsidered: Selected Papers from the English Institute*. New York: Columbia University Press, 1963.

Frye Northrop. "Emily Dickinson." In *Majcr Writers of America*. Ed. Perry Miller. New York: Harcourt, Brace, 1962. 5 Vols,

...... *The Educated Imagination*, Bloomington: Indiana University Press, 1971.

...... *The Secular Scripture: A Study of the Structure of Romance*. London: Harvard University Press, 1978.

...... *The Well-tempered Critic*, Bloomington: Indiana University Press, 1967.

Gelpi, Albert J. *Emilv Dickinson: The Mind of the Poet*. Mass. : Harvard University Press, 1965,

Gillespie, R. "Circumference of Emily Dickinson." *New English Quarterly*, 46 (1973), 250-71.

Graham, Desmond. "*Introduction to Poetry*. London: Oxford University Press, 1968.

Grant, Douglas. "The American Lyric." In *Purpose and Peace : Essays on American Writers*. New York: St. Martin's Press, 1965.

Greedman, Ralph. "Wallace Stevens and Rainer Maria Rilke: Two Versions of a Poetic." In *The Poet as Critic*. Ed. Frederick P.W. Mc Dowell. Evanston: Northwestern University Press, 1967.

Griffith, Clark. *The Long Shadow : Emily Dickinson's Tragic Poetry*. Princeton : Princeton University Press, 1964.

Gross, John F. "Tell All the Truth but——." *Ball State University Forum*, 10 (1969), 71-77.

Gross, Theodore. *The Heroic Ideal in American Literature*. New York : Free Press, 1971,

Happold, F.C. *Religious Faith and Twentieth-Century Man*. Penguin Books : Harmondsworth, 1966.

Harper's New Monthly Magazine. Vol. II, September 1851.

Helms, Randel. "Blake at Felpham : A Study in the Psychological Division." *Literature and Psychology*. Vol. XXII, No. 2 (1972), 57-66.

Heidegger, Martin. *An Introduction to Metaphysics.* Translated by Ralph Manheim. New York : Doubleday & Co., 1961.

Henderson, Joseph L. and Maud Oakes. *The Wisdom of the Serpent : The Myths of Death, Rebirth, and Resurrection.* New York: George Brazileer, 1963.

Higgins, David James Monroe. *Portrait of Emily Dickinson: The Poet and Her Prose.* New Brunswick: Rutgers University Press, 1967.

Higginson, M.W. *Letters and Journals of T.W. Higginson 1846-1906.* Ed. Mary Thracher Higginson. Boston: Houghton Mifflis, 1921.

Hillyer, Robert S. *In Pursuit of Poetry.* New York: Mc Graw Hill, 1960.

Hoffman, Daniel G., ed. *American Poetry and Poetics: Poems and Critical Documents from the Puritans to Robert Frost.* New York: Doubleday & Co., Anchor Books, 1962.

Hoffman, Frederick J. *The Mortal No: Death and the Modern Imagination.* Princeton: Princeton University Press, 1964.

Holmes, Theodore. "The Voice of Poet: The Art of Emily Dickinson." *Dalhansie Review,* 48 (1968-69), 551-55.

James, William. *The Varieties of Religious Experience.* Collins: Fontana Books, 1971.

Jenkins, Macgregor. *Emily Dickinson: A Friend and Neighbour.* Boston, 1930.

Jennings, Elizabeth. "Emily Dickinson and the Poetry of the Inner Life." *Review of English Literature,* 3 (1962), 78-87.

Johnson, T.H. *Emily Dickinson : An Interpretive Biography.* Cambridge, Mass. : Harvard University Press, 1963.

......*Final Harvest: Emily Dickinson's Poems.* Boston, 1961.

......*Emily Dickinson : A Collection of Critical Essays.* Ed. Richard B. Sewall. New Jersey: Prentice Hall, 1963.

Jones, Edmund D. *English Critical Essays: Nineteenth Century.* London: Oxford University Press, 1971.

Josephson, Matthew. "Those who Stayed." In *Portrait of the Artist in America.* New York: Harcourt, 1930.

Juhasz, Suzanne. " 'A Privilege so Awful': Emily Dickinson as Woman Poet." In *Naked and Fiery Forms: Modern American Poetry by Women, A New Tradition.* New York: Harper and Row, 1976, pp. 7-32.

Juhasz, Suzanne." 'I Dwell in Possibility': Emily Dickinson in the subjunctive Mood." *Emily Dickinson Bulletin 32* (June 1977) : 105-9.

Jung, C.G. "Psychology and Literature." In *Modern Man in Search of a Soul.* Translated by W.S. Dell and Cary F. Baynes. New York: Harcourt, Brace, & World, 1933.

......*Four Archetypes.* London: Routledge & Kegan Paul, 1972.

Kaul, A.N. *The American Vision: Actual and Ideal Society in Nineteenth Century Fiction.* New Haven: Yale University Press, 1963.

Kazin, Alfred, ed. *The Portable Blake.* New York: Viking Press, 1966.

Keleher, Julia. "The Enigma of Emily Dickinson." *New Mexico Quarterly*, II (November, 1932), 326-32.

Kermode, Frank. *Romantic Image.* Collins: Fortana Books, 1971.

Khan, Salamatullah. "The Love Poetry of Emily Dickinson." *The Literary Criterion,* 6 (Summer, 1964), 37-51.

......*Emily Dickinson's Poetry: The Flood Subjects.* New Delhi: Aarti Book Centre, 1969.

Kher, Inder Nath. *The Landscape of Absence: Emily Dickinson's Poetry.* New Haven: Yale University Press, 1974.

..... " 'An Abyss's Face' : The Structure of Emily Dickinson's Poem." *Emily Dickinson Bulletin,* 9 (June, 1969), 52-55.

Knight, Grant Cochran. *American Literature and Culture.* New York: Ray Lay, Rich and R. Smith, Inc.. 1936.

Langer, Susanne K. *Philosophy in a New Key; A Study in the Symbolism of Reason, Rite, and Art.* New York: New American Library, 1951.

......*Feeling and Form.* New York: Charles Scribner's Sons, 1953.

......*PhilosophicalSketches: A Study of the Human Mind in Relation to Feeling, Explored through Art, Language, and Symbol.* New York: New American Library, 1964.

Larson, Martin A. *The Religion of the Occident.* N. Jersey: Littlefield, Adams & Co., 1961.

Lawrence, D.H. *Selected Poems.* Ed. Kenneth Rerroth. New York: New Directions, 1947.

Lewis, H.D. *Our Experience of God.* Collins: Fontana Books 1970.

Leyda, Jay. "Late Thaw of a Frozen Image." *New Republic,* 132 (February, 1955). 22-24.

......*The Years and Hours of Emily Dickinson.* New Haven: Yale University press, 1960.

Lindberg-Seyersted Brita. "The Theme of Death in Emily Dickinson's-Poetry." *Studia Neophilologica,* 34 (1962), 269-81.

Lindberg-Seyersted, Brita. *The Voice of the Poet: Aspects of Style in the Poetry of Emily Dickinson.* Cambridge, Mass.: Harvard University Press, 1968.

Longsworth, Polly. *Emily Dickinson: Her Letter to the World.* New York: Crowell, 1965.

Lowell, Amy. "Emily Dickinson." In *Poetry and Poets.* Boston: Houghton Mifflin Co., 1930.

Lubbers, Klaus. *Emily Diokinson: The Critical Revolntion.* Ann Arbor: University of Miehigan Press, 1968.

Lucas, Dolores Dyer. *Emily Dickinson and Riddle.* Northern Illinois University Press, 1969.

Luisi, David. "Some Aspects of Emily Dickinson's Food Liquor Poems." *English Studies,* 52 (1971), 32-40.

MacLeish, Archibald; Bogan, Louise; and, Wilbur, Richard. *Emily Dickinson: Three Views.* Foreword by Reginald F. French. Amherst: Amherst College Press,1960.

MacLeish Archibald. "The Private World: Poems of Emily Dickin son." *Personalist*, 43 (1962), 497-514.

......*Poetry and Experience*. Boston: Houghton, Mifflin Co., Riverside Press, 1961.

McNaughton, Ruth Flanders. *The Imagery of Emily Dickinson*. University of Necraska Studies, new series, no. 4. Lincoln: University of Nebraska Press,1949.

Marka, Ballanger. "The Metaphysical Echo. "*English Studies in Africa*, VIII (March, 1965).

Martin, Jay. "Emily Dickinson." In *Harvests of Change: American Literature 1865-1914*. New Jersey: Prentice Hall, 1967.

Martz, Louis L. "Donne and the Meditative Tradition'." *Thought*, XXXIV (Summer, 269-78).

......"Whitman and Dickinson: Two Aspects of the Self." In *The Poems of the Mind: Essays on Poetry, English and American*. New York: Oxford University Press, 1966.

Matthiessen, F.O. "The Problem of the Private Poet." *Kenyon Review*, 7 (1945), 584-97.

McCarthy, Paul. "An Approach to Dickinson's Poetry." *Emerson Society Quarterly*, 44 (1966), 22-31.

McElderry, B.R. Jr. "Emily Dickinson: Viable Transcendentalst" *Emerson Society Quarterly*, 44 (1966) 17-21.

McSweeney K. "Melville, Dickinson Whitman and Psychoanalytic Criticism. "*Critical Quarterly*, 19 (September, 1977), 71-82.

Miller, F. De Wolfe. "Emily Dickinson's Assumption of Aristocratic Values." PMLA, LXXVII, No. 2 (May, 1962).

Miller, James E. Jr. "Emily Dickinson: The Thunder's Tongue." *Minnesota Review*, 2 (1962), 289-304.

Miller, Perry. "From Edwards to Emerson." *New England Quarterly*, XIII (December, 1940), 617.

......*The New England Mind*. Boston, 1961, 2 Vols.

......*The Transcendentalists*. Cambridge : Harvard University Press, 1967.

......*The American Puritans*. New York : Doubleday & Co., Inc., 1956.

Miller, J. Hillis. *The Disappearance of God*. Cambridge : Harvard University Press. 1963.

Miller, Ruth. *The Poetry of Emily Dickinson*. Middle Town, Wesleyan Univ. Press, 1968.

Miller, F.D. "Emily Dickinson : Self Portrait in the Third Person". *New English Quarterly*, 46 (March, 1973), 119-24.

Mudge, Jean McClure. *Emily Dickinson : the Image of Home*. Amherst : University of Massachusetts Press, 1975.

Neill O' Judith. *Critics on Blake*. London : Hutchinson & Co. Ltd., 1970.

Ninde, Edward. *The Story of the American Hymn*. New York : the Abingdon Press, 1921.

Oliver, Egbert S. *Studies in American Literature*, New Delhi : Eurasia Publishing House, 1971.

Ossole, Margaret Fuller. *Women in the Nineteenth Century*. Boston: Houghton, 1951.

Patterson, Rebecca. "Emily Dickinson's Double Time : Masculine Identification." *American Image*, 28 (Winter, 1971), 330-62.

..... *The Riddle of Emily Dickinson*. Boston : Houghton,Mifflin Co., 1951.

Pickard, John B. *Emily Dickinson : An Introduction and Interpretation*. New York : Holt, 1967.

Pollak, V.R. "That Fine Prosperity : Economic Metaphors in Emily Dickinson's Poetry." *Modern Language Quarterly*; 34 (1973), 161-79.

Pollitt, Josephine. *Emily Dickinson: The Human Background of Her Poetry*. New York : Copper Square Publishers, 1970.

Poster, David Thomas. *The Art of Emily Dickinson's Early Poetry*. Cambridge, Harvard University Press, 1966.

Power, Sister Mary James. *In the Name of the Bee : The Significance of Emily Dickinson*. New York : Sheed & Ward, 1944.

Pritchard, John Paul. *Criticism in America*. Ludhiana : Lyall Book Depot, 1970.

Proetz, Victor. "Onward and Upward with the Arts." *The Astonishment of Words*. New Yorker, 47 (May 22, 1971), 82-121.

Read, Herbert. *Poetry and Experience*. Clarke, Double & Brendon Ltd., 1967.

......*The Meaning of Art*. Penguin Books : Harmondsworth, 1956.

Reeves, James, ed. *Selected Poems*. London : Heineman, 1959.

Richards, I.A. *Principles of Literary Criticism*. London : Routledge & Kegan Paul, 1955.

Resenbaum, S. P. *A. Concordance to the Poems of Emily Dickinson*. New York : Cornea University Press, 1964.

Schwartz, Elias. *The Forms of Feeling : Toward a Mimetic Theory of Literature*. London : Kennikat Press, 1972.

Scribner's monthly. Vol. II, November 1875 to April 1876. New York : Scribner's and Co.

Sebeok, Thomas A. *Myth, a Symposium*. Bloomington : Indiana University Press, 1972.

Sewall, Richard Benson. *The Life of Emily Dickinson*. New York, 1974.

Sewall, Richard Benson. *The Lyman Letters : New Light on Emily Dickinson and Her Family*, Amherst : University of Mass. Press. 1965.

......*Emily Dickinson : A Collection of Critical Essays*. New Jersey : Prentice-Hall, 1963.

Sherwood, William R. *Circumference aud Circumstance : Stages in the Mind and Art of Emily Dickinson*. New York : Columbia Uuiversity Press. 1968.

Springer, Marlene. "Emily Dickinson's Humorous Road to Heaven." *Renascence*, 23, (1971), 129-36.

Stewart, Randall. *American Literature and Christian Doctrine*. Louisiana State University Press, 1958.

Taggard, Genevieve. *The Life and Mind of Emily Dickinson.* New York : Alfred A. Knof, 1934.

Todd, John Emerson. *Emily Dickinson's use of Persona.* The Hague, 1973.

Thackrey, Donald E. *Emily Dickinson's Approach ta Poetry.* University of Nebraska Studies, New series, no. 13. Lincoln: University of Nebraska Press, 1954.

Tomlinson, Charles, ed. *Marianne Moore : A Collection of Critical Essays.* New Jersey : Englewood Cliffs, 1969.

Untermeyer, Louis B. *Modern American poetry.* New York : Harcourt, 1921.

Van Doren, Carl. *American Literature : An Introduction.* Los Angeles : Westwood Hills Press, 1933.

Vermon, Maint. *Emily Dickinson : Love Poems and Others.* New York, 1952.

Waggner, Hyatt H. "Emily Dickinson : the Transcendental Self." *American Poets from the Puritans to the Present.* Boston : Houghton, 1968.

Walsh, John Evangelist. *The Hidden Life of Emily Dickinson.* New York : Simon, 1971.

Ward, Theodora. *The Capsule of the Mind : Chapters in the Life of Emily Dickinson.* Cambridge, Mass. : Harvard University Press, 1961.

Warren, Austen. *The New England Conscience.* Ann Arbor : University of Michigan Press, 1966.

Watts, Alan W. *The Two Hands of God : the Myths of Polarity.* New York, 1963.

Waugh, Dorothy. *Emily Dickinson's Beloved, A Surmise.* New York : Vantage Press, 1975.

Weisbuch, Robert. *Emily Dickinson's Poetry.* Chicago : University of Chicago Press, 1975.

Wells Henry, W. *Introduction to Emily Dickinson*, Chicago : Packard & Co., 1947.

Wells, Henry Willis. *New Poets from Old : A Study in Literary Genetics.* New York : Columbia University Press, 1940.

......*Introduction to Emily Dickinson.* New York : Hendricks House 1959.

Whicher, G.F. "Poetry After the Civil War." In *American Writers on American Literature.* Ed. John Macy, New York, 1931,

......*This was a Poet : a Critical Biography of Emily Dickinson.* New York : Scribner, 1938.

Whiting, Lilian. *The World Beautiful in Books.* Boston, 1901.

Wilder, Amos N. *Eschatology and Ethics in the Teaching of Jesus.* New York : Harper & Bros,, 1950.

Willard, Dennis S.R. "Emily Dickinson and her 'Letter to the World'."

In *The Experience in American Literature*. Ed. Carl Brde. New York, 1961.

Williams, Oscar, ed. *A Pocket Book of Modern Verse*. New York : Washington Square Press, Inc., 1967.

Wilner, Eleanor, "The Poetics of Emily Dickinson." *Journal of English Literary History*, 38 (1971), 262-64.

Wilson, Colin. *The Outsider*, London : Pan Books Ltd., 1971.

Wilson, Colin. *Poetry and Mysticism*. London : Hutchinson & Co., Ltd., 1970.

Wylder, Edith, *The Latest Face* : *Emily Dickinson's Manuscripts*. Albuquerque : University of New Mexico Press, 1971.

Index of Dickinson Poems Discussed

(The number of the poem is within brackets with the page numbers following.)

GENERAL INDEX